ALBERT SCHWEITZER'S GIFT OF FRIENDSHIP

ERICA ANDERSON

Albert Schweitzer's
Gift of Friendship

HARPER & ROW, PUBLISHERS

NEW YORK,
EVANSTON,
AND LONDON

Photographs by the author appear on pages 25-40 and 105-120.

Foreword

Leaving the Lambaréné airport on June 6, 1964, I asked the pilot to alter his course slightly and circle over the Schweitzer Hospital before turning toward Libreville on the first leg of my journey to New York. He kindly consented to my wish and for a brief moment I was able to have a last look at the red roofs, the plantation, the leper village, the jungle clearing so dear to me.

An hour earlier I had stood in the boat taking me across the Ogowe River, waving to Dr. Schweitzer and the group of people who had accompanied me down to the landing to say good-by.

Eighteen times I had been in Lambaréné since my visit in March, 1951, when we first met and when, though I did not know it then, the friendship with Dr. Schweitzer took root. I did not know then that friendships with Schweitzer are born and ripen as naturally as healthy seeds grow when they are planted in good earth and tended with care.

He is never aloof, he is always available—open, warm, concerned for each of those who seek him out, accepting them into his life. My experience is far from unique: I am but one of a great many who are indebted to Dr. Schweitzer for the privilege of knowing him as a friend.

January 14, 1965, marks the ninetieth anniversary of his birth. This book, which tells of the times I was able to spend with him in Africa and in Europe, is a token of my unending gratitude that

he allowed me, an intruder, to fulfill my dream of making a film
of his life and work to present to all those who would never meet
him or reach the Lambaréné hospital. That hospital has been
the scene of healing for every sort of pain, of spirit as well as of
body. For me the meeting with Dr. Schweitzer in Lambaréné was
a turning point, as it has been for countless others. The personal
encounter with the daily witness of his life brings home with great
force the depth and wisdom of his philosophy, and strengthens
the conviction that its wider acceptance could create the new spirit
of humanity for which the world longs.

E. A.

1

I HAD SCARCELY HEARD of Dr. Albert Schweitzer until a winter evening in 1949, when I went down to a bookstore at Grand Central Station in New York City to pick up a book for a friend of mine. Snow had been falling all day, and the city was covered with a thick white blanket. There were no cabs around. I walked. The streets were hushed, almost deserted, and I enjoyed the stroll from my apartment on Central Park West. Such leisure was a rare treat for me in those days, as I was buried deep in documentary film work, cooped up all day in cutting rooms, rushing out for quick meals, and not returning home until after midnight.

At the bookstore, while the clerk was getting my friend's book, I began to browse about, and a photograph caught my eye. It was the first picture of Dr. Schweitzer I'd ever seen. Something within me said: "*This* is for you. This you must read." In fact, the feeling I had to have that book was so strong that, had anyone tried to take it from me, I believe I would have fought for it with my fists.

Fortunately, no practical proof of my determination was called for. The clerk gladly sold me the Schweitzer book—his autobiography—along with the other, but I did not read it that night— or even that winter. I wanted to wait until I had more time, more leisure. I put it on the bookshelf above my bed, where I'd often look at it as I sank into bed, dead-tired.

The next summer I finished my film, and one hot Saturday, as I was starting out for the beach with some friends, I took Dr. Schweitzer's autobiography with me. Once I'd started it, I never even went in swimming. Once I'd finished it, I said good-by to my friends, went straight home, and read it through again. I was in a spell, and immediately wrote a letter to Dr. Schweitzer:

Dear and esteemed Doctor Schweitzer:

I found your autobiography—I cannot describe how this book has captivated me! I have read it twice. I cannot help but thank you! To know about your work, your thoughts and your life is a present, forever renewing itself. Your life is an answer to so many questions. How shall I thank you?

I am filled with the profound desire to make a documentary film of your life and work. It would mean so much to me to be granted permission to take films of your hospital and of you, to try to capture the atmosphere and reality of your work and to bring it to hundreds and thousands of people, those who might never have a chance to meet you.

I am from Vienna, but I have lived in America for almost ten years. All this time I have made documentary films. For example, one of the British sculptor, Henry Moore, another one of French tapestries when they were exhibited here, one of the American primitive painter, Grandma Moses, one for the Red Cross and one for the Humane Society. These films are being shown in schools, colleges, universities and clubs all over the U.S.A.

Forgive this direct letter to you but I see a documentary film of your work so alive in front of me and am so deeply convinced of the good which a visual record could do for those who see it. I believe such a film could also create financial support for your hospital, because I would, I feel sure, be able to arrange that the income through distribution of the film would go to the hospital.

I don't want to take up your valuable time and go into details. I only ask you whether you would, on principle, be for such a project. And this too: The conception of this film would be entirely subject to your approval. Indeed it would only be possible to do it if you would agree and give your consent and co-operation.

Dear Doctor Schweitzer, if you are for such a document, please let me know. I feel sure I can raise the necessary funds for this undertaking if you believe with me in the good such a film could do.

That my whole heart and admiration is yours I need not stress. I am sad that at the time of your visit to America I was working on a film in Europe and could not meet you. Forgive again that I took the liberty of writing this letter but, really, I had no choice. I had to tell you that I am burning with this wish; you are the source and origin of it!

Impatiently I wait for your kind answer and hope with all my heart that you will not refuse this idea.

In gratitude and admiration,

Erica Anderson

I went about my business, but anybody, whether they wanted to listen to me or not, invariably heard me ramble on about Schweitzer and, in my optimism, I mentioned that I was "only waiting" for his consent in order to embark on this new and exciting venture.

Months and months went by, but I received no answer.

By that time I was in Switzerland with Jerome Hill, a talented movie director and producer, working on a film biography of the noted psychiatrist Professor Carl G. Jung. Jerome was also enthusiastic about making a film on Schweitzer, but, being more realistic than I, urged me not to go overboard until I got a definite answer. Each day I'd work with Professor Jung on the lake in Bollingen until late in the evening, when I'd return to my hotel in Zürich. One evening the hotel clerk handed me a message which read: "Call Mrs. Clara Urquhart." Not knowing a soul in Zürich, I thought it was some mistake. It was not.

It turned out that all my talking about the Schweitzer project had not been in vain, after all. A California friend of mine knew a lady in Switzerland who had helped Dr. Schweitzer in his work for many years and who had become his close friend. That lady was Clara Urquhart. My friend had contacted her on my behalf, and now I held her message in my hand.

Clara Urquhart received me graciously the following day. Although we were complete strangers, I immediately felt as though we had been lifetime friends. She was on my side about the film project, but cautioned me against being overoptimistic.

"Many friends of his, including myself, have tried to convince him of the value of such a film," she told me. "But he's always refused."

My heart sank.

"Don't give up, though," she added cheerfully. "With Schweitzer, one never knows. Perhaps he will listen to you."

At that point she was called to the phone. When she returned there was a smile on her face.

"I believe your project is under a lucky star," she told me. "That was Mme. Emmy Martin. She's an old friend of Dr. Schweitzer and his European representative. She'll be in Zürich tomorrow. She doesn't come often. You must meet her and maybe show her one of your films."

We showed Mme. Martin my Grandma Moses film, and she

liked its simplicity; but she made no secret of her opposition to a film about the Doctor. She was worried that it would prove too much of a strain and distraction from his work, especially for a man his age. Moreover, she enlightened me on another discouraging fact: that almost all the major American film companies had at one time or another approached Dr. Schweitzer and offered him huge sums of money for the hospital in return for permission to make a film. He had turned them all down.

My optimism took another nose dive—but not my enthusiasm. Hollywood, I pointed out, would probably have sent hundreds of people swarming all over Lambaréné with tons of camera equipment, whereas I planned to go out there alone. Wouldn't this be in my favor? I pleaded with Mme. Martin just to put in a good word for me.

Although she later was very helpful, at this point Mme. Martin remained deadset against the whole idea. Clara, however, promised to pass on another letter of mine to Dr. Schweitzer so that it would at least reach him personally. She thought it was questionable whether the first letter had even come to his attention.

A month later I opened, with trembling hands, a letter from Africa:

My dear Mrs. Erica Anderson,

A thousand thanks for your letter with the kind offer to make a documentary film of my life and my work, and with it to create a source of financial support for the hospital. Oh, I fully appreciate the value of a film, and yet, sorry as I am, I cannot consent to your plan.

The main reason is that a film of my life and of my hospital would be a difficult, an almost impossible task. There would be no action, no plot, only a series of disconnected scenes which offer nothing for the eye. And how difficult it would be to capture the activities of the hospital on film!

In 1938 M. Poirier made a documentary film on the life of Brazza. At that time I learned about all the difficulties of such an undertaking. With the insufficient light of the continually covered equatorial sky you may sometimes have to wait ten days before you can take pictures for a quarter of an hour! That's how it is in the tropical climate of Equatorial Africa . . .

Therefore listen to me. Give up this adventurous plan to film here. It would mean nothing but worry and disillusionment. It is hard for me to have to tell you this, but there is no other way about it. Oh, really, I have often let this idea of a film go through my mind—the conclusion was always the same.

Devotedly,
Albert Schweitzer

"This is it," I thought. The answer was a resounding "No." And yet on a close look, his negative reply was based entirely on the obstacles *I* was likely to encounter. After all, he talked only about technical problems—things that were in my domain. Surely I would lick them! I was not going to give up so easily. My first impulse was to draw up a reply immediately. I had asked for his permission, not his advice on technical difficulties! I felt stubborn, almost angry.

Of course at that time I was not familiar with Dr. Schweitzer's ways. I did not know then that, in his concern for others, he would sincerely think of the hardships the other fellow had to face. On the other hand, I didn't realize how personally opposed he was to my project. Only much later did I find out that he had written Clara Urquhart at the same time: "I would rather burn in hell than have a film made of my life."

With all my initial enthusiasm I also had the idea that all I would need to produce a neat little film would be four weeks of shooting, two in Lambaréné and two in Europe. Even allowing ample time for editing and sound synchronization, I thought the picture could be completed in about six months. Had somebody told me then, "It will take you seven years to make this film," I would have thought it ridiculous. And yet the truth is that when the film was finished at last, my greatest regret was that I could not spend another seven years on it.

Anyway, I drafted another letter to Dr. Schweitzer, telling him that, instead of discouraging me, his answer had only made me all the more determined to overcome the very obstacles he had cited. I closed:

"Your time is so valuable. Don't go to the trouble of answering me at length. Just send me one word—'yes' (I hope and pray) or 'no,' if you are really convinced that I must not attempt to realize my dream."

Once more I waited. I could not admit the possibility of a refusal. In the meantime I read all the books by and about Dr. Schweitzer that I could lay my hands on. I became more fascinated

5 ᢒᢀ

than ever, and more involved. It dawned on me that I'd probably been wrong to prescribe such a tight time limit for the film. Already I saw so much material to be researched, so many fields of Schweitzer's interests to be explored. In the light of his philosophy, my own life had assumed a new meaning, a fresh dimension. Even the delay made sense: I needed time to learn, to become ready.

When friends teased me about my "forthcoming African trip," I would answer with grim determination, "I am waiting," whereupon they would smile indulgently. Once I confided to a close friend of mine: "When I say I'm waiting, I think I just make believe, to conceal my disappointment. But then again, when I ask myself in the stillness of the night, 'Shall I ever be permitted to make that film?' the answer from the depth of my heart is 'Yes.'"

Just before Christmas of 1950 another letter from Africa arrived. I tore the envelope open. This time the handwriting was not his.

Dr. Schweitzer has asked me to write to you. He is burdened by his extensive correspondence and by the many visitors who travel as far as Lambaréné. He is distressed because he cannot find the time to finish the books on which, he feels, he ought to work. He has written you what he thinks of your plans for a motion picture. You are but one of many whom he has asked to drop their plans, and he cannot and will not change his mind. In addition to the reasons he mentioned to you himself, he could not give you the permission he has already denied old friends of his. . . . I realize how great will be your disappointment, but measured against the disappointments the Doctor has had to suffer in the course of his life, I am sure that yours can be overcome. Please forgive me that I, as an old co-worker of Dr. Schweitzer's, have to transmit this refusal. I always feel much happier when I can pass on something positive. . . .

I was nearing the end of the page. My heart was sinking. But at the very bottom I saw two lines:

Come. But not to film. I cannot go back on my decision. I cannot grant you what I have refused others. I cannot.

These words, written in Dr. Schweitzer's own hand, were signed: "With my best thoughts, Albert Schweitzer."
Here was something to keep my hopes alive. But it was no

more than that. "Come," he said. But how could I afford to go to Africa without a chance of returning with a film?

I talked the matter over with Jerome Hill. To my immense joy, he volunteered to finance the trip anyway. It was his belief that a personal talk with Dr. Schweitzer might accomplish what further letters could not. I cabled Dr. Schweitzer my grateful acceptance of his invitation. The rest was in God's hands.

There was no further word from Africa, so I plunged into preparations for the trip and dreamed of my first meeting with the famous Doctor. But beneath all my excitement there was a cold undercurrent of doubt and fear. I was expected in Lambaréné strictly as a visitor. My profession, my cameras, my tools—all these I was supposed to leave behind. I could not disobey the command of the Doctor; yet without my equipment, what chance did I have to succeed.

Jerome professed great confidence in my powers of persuasion, but I was terrified by the prospect of failure. Again and again I would say to Jerome: "He will think I am deaf and dumb. I won't even be able to open my mouth when I meet him."

All this kept churning around in my head. Waking and sleeping I could think of nothing else. As the day of my departure drew nearer, I was haunted by wild nightmares in which elephants would toss me about on their tusks, tigers would tear me to shreds, and swarms of mosquitoes would bite me raw. But worse was my recurrent dream of being rejected by Dr. Schweitzer and his staff. I'd see myself walking among white-clad doctors, nurses, and aides, who would coldly turn their backs on me when I'd start to speak.

One day I had another unexpected stroke of good luck. A collector of African art, Ladislaus Segy, asked me whether I could shoot some background footage for him in the Congo, since he was considering making a film about African woodcarvings. I was delighted. It was another link in the chain of little miracles: first, my meeting with Clara Urquhart, then Jerome Hill's commitment, and now this ideal excuse for lugging my camera equipment to Lambaréné. But I decided not to inform Dr. Schweitzer of this new development. I did not want to push my luck too far, and, besides, I felt somewhat guilty about it.

Now that I was to travel loaded down with cameras, tripods, and cases of film, Jerome decided I should have Julia Knowlton, a film editor I had worked with before, come to assist. This raised another complication. Schweitzer had invited me alone. Would he have room to accommodate both of us? Was it right to keep this a secret too? By this time my optimism was soaring high again, and I decided that Julia's presence, as well as that of the cameras, could best be explained when we got there. My ideas about Lambaréné were so hazy that I planned to leave Julia, along with all the luggage, at some little "conveniently located hotel," and then present myself alone at the hospital "during visiting hours." We even decided not to notify Dr. Schweitzer in advance of our arrival, which resulted in the first of a long series of black marks I earned during my first days in Africa.

2

ON MARCH 3, 1951, Julia and I take off from Idlewild. I am so relieved to be on the way at last that I doze off; but the face of Dr. Schweitzer appears in a dream. His eyes, instead of having the familiar kindly expression, glare at me fiercely. "I don't want a film!" he shouts. "You know that! Why do you keep pursuing me?"

At Amsterdam, we change planes for Brazzaville, the capital of French Equatorial Africa, and, after an hour or so, approach the Swiss Alps. The sun glitters on the silent, snow-capped mountaintops, so forbidding and yet so peaceful . . . I take a few shots with my Rolleiflex . . . Clouds sail below the highest peaks. We fly over lower mountains, down into the valleys of Italy. Then Rome: a glimpse of the Old Stadium, the Coliseum. We land there, but, to my dismay, have no time to visit the city. The warm sun is very welcome after the cold winds of Amsterdam.

We reboard the plane at six in the evening, and night falls quickly. For hours I look into the deep sky above, the stars shining all around us. One does feel nearer to them at twenty thousand feet up. We cross the Sahara, but cannot see the desert sands. Julia sleeps soundly beside me, and eventually I fall asleep too . . . I awake with a start, the plane is descending over thousands of small lights. It's the native village of Kano, we are told, where lights are kept on all through the night to scare off the wild animals. When we land, it is strange to stand on African soil for the first time, and to watch the natives, barefooted, barewaisted, the red fez on their heads, jump on the wings of the plane and refuel the engines.

An old Chevrolet truck careens us to the KLM guesthouse about three hundred yards from the landing field. There a market is in full swing. Natives squat on the ground, trying to sell cheap alligator bags, ivory carvings, scarves, and flamboyant materials. It's all a bit commercial, but I can hardly resist the native boys chanting: "Lady, lady, buy bargain. Is cheap, is beautiful."

Julia and I sit down and order cool drinks. All around us broken-up conversations start among the other passengers, so typical of stop-offs at strange airports early in the morning. Everyone is slightly lonely, their eyes heavy with sleep, yet eager to exchange their first impressions. What is Africa *really* like? Does the heat make you sick? Are there really so many mosquitoes? Can one avoid dysentery? Do you have to take pills against malaria?

At Brazzaville, where we're supposed to change planes for the last lap of our journey, it turns out that we won't be able to make connections for at least six days! On top of that, the hotels are all full, and we are lucky to find a room, even for one night. We are so tired and dirty from the trip, but there's no hot water. In our condition, though, even the cold shower is refreshing. While we're resting, there is a sudden downpour. Outside, natives hurry by, half naked, rain puddles quickly turn to lakes, the water rushes down the roofs in cascades. For the first time I believe we are actually in Africa.

When the rain lets up, we take a ferry across the Congo to Leopoldville, where we hope to find rooms for the rest of our stay. The ferry boat is a small motor launch, very crowded. When I try to get in with the natives, they shout at me wildly and point to a sign: WHITES IN FRONT, COLORED IN THE REAR. Between Brazzaville and Leopoldville, the Congo is so wide it is barely possible to see the opposite shore on a clear day. The river water is dirty yellow, filled with trash, bushes, flowers, pieces of woven basket. We learn that the water lilies are a serious hazard to shipping, sometimes choking up the whole river.

Leopoldville is much livelier than Brazzaville. I'm impressed by the posture of the native women. Their bodies, whether fat or slim, have so much movement in their colorful drapes. Some are bare above the waist and nurse their babies while they walk, talk, bargain, or argue.

We make arrangements to stay at the Hotel Regina—but only for one night—and after lunch we call up an American friend of mine who has lived in the Congo for many years. She picks us up in a Cadillac, and we drive through the native village, very dirty and smelly, along the banks of the Congo to the hills overlooking the rapids. In the white residential section, the houses are large, airy, and comfortable. My friend tells us that most white women have become extremely lazy and spoiled while living in Africa. They have lots of colored servants—mostly male—looking after the housework. She has five herself—one just for ironing! She acts very surly with her own help, but she claims it's essential—there are more than twenty natives in Leopoldville for every white man. After nine in the evening, there's a curfew for all the natives. They are allowed out only with a special pass—very difficult to obtain. My friend admits that the whites, underneath their harshness, are scared of an uprising and feign more self-assurance than they actually feel. I thought, what a relief it will be to meet Albert Schweitzer who went to Africa to serve—not to exploit—the natives.

We visit the market with the help of a local guide. Gingerly, he leads us through throngs of people. The women balance their wares on their heads, walking sure-footed even with heavy loads. Generally the natives, shy and scared of my camera, hide, turn away, or run. The market place is filthy; children's noses are running, their bodies are covered with bites, and wherever they are they make puddles, or worse.

We find a room for the night at a small guesthouse—a second- or third-rate affair. Even the linen on the beds is dirty—to say nothing of the toilet facilities. I look forward to the coziness of the mosquito netting, but ours are full of holes, and impossible to repair, they are so large. And yet the room is terribly expensive. Everything in Leopoldville seems twice as expensive as in the States, with the one exception of labor, which is cheap and exploited.

After getting settled for our one-night stand, we take a taxi down to the rapids of the Congo. It is four o'clock, but the sun is still shining full blast. The air is very humid. We cross the Pont Léon, a hanging bridge precariously supported by crude piles driven into the ground. Every third or fourth step is missing. A group of naked children, their brown bodies glistening in the sun, frolic in the running water. Unlike their elders, they're delighted to be photographed, and clown around, making such a racket their voices can be heard above the falls. A hundred yards farther on, we reach the falls and come upon two girls and two boys amusing themselves under the palm trees. The girls are furious at our intrusion; but the boys do not mind being photographed— but for a price! Naïvely, I offer them a dollar, but they want two, and it takes a lot of gestures to convince them one is my limit. When they know I mean it, though, they relax and decide to tag along after us. Then the younger children join us, and we must look like a safari, working our way along the riverbank with our many followers. It is always this way in Africa, I learn later; the natives love to follow strangers around, out of curiosity, out of the hope that some presents may turn up for them, but mainly because they have all the time in the world. I'm only sorry the boys are so fond of Western clothing—their own native garb is more colorful. Suddenly, one of the youngsters dives in the river and disappears. Worried, I cry out, and the rest of the party laughs at my fear: downstream, the boy surfaces, a huge fish wiggling in his arms, which, reluctantly, I am persuaded to buy.

We stop at a small restaurant near the ferry, where we encounter a young American from Columbus, Ohio, a big game hunter; but he assures us that he hunts only for zoos, not to kill. He's arranging a huge safari of a thousand natives, not far from Lambaréné, to hunt for gorillas, tigers, and lions. His story sounds to me like something out of a romantic novel, and my eyes must have betrayed my thoughts, for he starts to pull out all kinds of credentials to prove his identity.

When he learns why we are in Africa, it isn't long before he asks us to join him, after our Lambaréné visit, to photograph his hunting trip. It seems that a fight between a lion and a crocodile has never been filmed before! I get all excited—until he informs us that he charges visitors on his safaris eight hundred dollars a week!

"But you two," he adds generously, "I would take along for nothing. It would be a pleasure. All you'd need to bring is some salt and gunpowder for the natives."

He emphasizes that time in Africa does not exist.

"The first time I came I planned to stay seven weeks," he tells us. "I stayed seven months. The next time I planned for seven months, and stayed two years. Never give yourself a time limit. Sometimes it takes me a week just to contact the bush people. When I first arrive with a safari, they hide. I leave a present for them on a tree trunk—a little gunpowder, or tobacco. The next day it will be gone, and I repeat the procedure. A few days later, if I'm lucky, I'll find a present they've left for me in the same spot—a basket of fruit or an alligator skin. When I take it, the natives shyly start to appear, one by one, and we can start a palaver. Some of the bush people are really wild, though, and cannibalism still exists. With a good guide you are safe. Otherwise . . ." And he rolls his eyes toward heaven.

Back at the hotel we relax on the terrace and enjoy a faint breeze. At the next table sits a timid-looking lady. When she gets up to leave, her handkerchief falls to the floor.

"Madame, votre mouchoir!" I call out.

She picks it up.

"Considering that I am from Scotland, I think it is funny to be addressed in French," she says.

We ask her to join us for dinner and learn she is on her way to visit a friend in Rhodesia. Her trip from London has been a series of delays, breakdowns, and flight cancelations. She's never been out of Scotland before, her time is running out, and she's scared to take anything but tea in so dangerous a place as Africa.

We straighten her out about "time" in the Congo, and go to bed quite smugly, feeling like veteran African explorers, compared to the lady from Scotland.

3

THE MORNING of our departure we are waiting to board the plane when we learn to our horror that the Leopoldville newspaper has published an article about two ladies from America, loaded down with camera equipment, who are on their way to make a movie in Lambaréné. Loaded down with camera equipment! If Schweitzer has seen the story, I am sure we are finished before we start.

Our plane is an old and dilapidated Junker. It has no seats—just two rows of bunks—and our only traveling companions are three dead goats. For five hours we fly over huge jungle trees. The roof of green is impenetrable, and I cannot visualize what it covers. Suddenly we swoop down over a winding river—the Ogowe: we are landing in Lambaréné. I strain my neck: where is the hospital? As we touch ground on a flat meadow, not even an airstrip, I'm overcome by a wave of panic. The meeting with Schweitzer is now inescapable. My courage has hit rock bottom.

Natives rush forward to put up the ramp. We collect our baggage and are immediately confronted, as we step on land, by a young Frenchman who introduces himself as the Chief of the District. In broken English he informs us that Dr. Schweitzer is expecting us.

"Expecting us?" I counter in broken French. "Why, he doesn't even know we're arriving today."

"Perhaps not," says the Frenchman. "But he has been sending out a canoe every day for the past week. He did not wish to risk your being stranded on your arrival."

I am so embarrassed that I want to rush off and hide in the jungle. Here I am with an extra uninvited person, plus twenty-five pieces of luggage, and there's no way out but straight to the hospital. We are rushed into a jeep and driven over a dusty, bumpy road to the river's edge, where a dug-out canoe—a pirogue —is waiting.

Six native paddlers help to load our paraphernalia onto the boat. For the first time I meet lepers. Their sores, their maimed limbs, cut me to the quick. One has only half a foot left, another's fingers are crippled, and still another has no fingers at all. We glide silently along on the fast-moving current of the river. The men seem very friendly. They chatter all the while, smile at us, and paddle expertly, despite their physical handicaps.

We turn a bend and see across the river the famous landing of the Lambaréné hospital. The oarsmen now begin a rhythmic chant.

"This is the signal that we have you," one explains in pidgin French.

"Please don't sing," I plead with him. "We would like to arrive in silence."

"*Non, non, le Grand Docteur* very sad if we don't obey orders," he says with a laugh. "*Il est triste . . .*"

"Sad?" I say to Julia. "Not cross?"

"Don't worry—he'll be plenty cross with us, all right," she replies, delivering another blow to my morale.

To my great relief I see only one female figure on the landing as we extricate ourselves from the baggage. She introduces herself as Mlle. Emma Hausknecht, a nurse who has been with Dr. Schweitzer for over thirty years. She, too, is Alsatian, and her blue eyes sparkle with warmth as she welcomes us. Mlle. Emma does not waste one word on our luggage, and I am grateful at least that I don't have to explain it right away. She leads us past primitive-looking huts toward the building where we are to stay. The six paddlers, each balancing several pieces of our equipment on his head, follow us in solemn procession, and we make a rather conspicuous entrance.

"Your house is called *Sans Souci*," Mlle. Emma explains.

There is not much to be seen of the hospital itself as we climb uphill; all I notice in my bewilderment are lots of people roaming around, and with them, dogs, cats, goats, sheep, and a few little monkeys.

Mlle. Emma opens the door to our room. It's about nine by twelve feet, and one wall is screened in. It seems cool and pleasant after the climb.

"Make yourselves comfortable," she says, "and I'll go and announce your arrival to Dr. Schweitzer."

I sink into the only chair in the room, and Julia stretches out on a bed.

"I think I have a sunstroke already," she moans.

There are just two iron beds, a table, one small mirror, a washstand, two glasses, and some towels. Nothing else. Every other available space in the room is taken up with my camera equipment.

"Erica, where on earth is the ladies' room?" asks Julia. "I know neither French nor German, so you'll have to ask the questions for both of us."

I become quite annoyed with Julia.

"Here we have traveled thousands of miles," I tell her. "We're about to experience the most important moment in our lives, and all you can think about is finding the ladies' room. Are you out of your mind? I must get ready to face Dr. Schweitzer. I have to find the right words to explain your presence, the cameras . . ."

There is a knock at the door. A tall slim nurse enters, stands erect at the threshold, and scans the numerous pieces of luggage strewn around.

"So you did bring the cameras, after all?"

I can only stammer with embarrassment.

"Well, please hide it all under the beds," she goes on, more warmly. "And you shouldn't mention the film to Dr. Schweitzer now. He is very tired. As soon as you are ready, you may go and see him. He'll be waiting to welcome you."

"Let's go *now,* Julia. This is it." I start for the door.

"No!" Julia protests. "First you *must* find out about the ladies' room. That's your first duty. Then we can concentrate on meeting Dr. Schweitzer." Julia is making desperate signs, and, reluctantly, I ask for directions.

"Yes, of course," the nurse says. "I'll show you the way. We call it *Hinterindien* in German, meaning 'behind India' because it is far behind all the other buildings. Come along."

We step out of the room and—there is Dr. Schweitzer coming toward us, his hand outstretched.

He is wonderfully rugged looking. With his wild mustache and his massive frame, he gives the impression of great strength and power. We shake hands, but before I can utter a syllable, the nurse informs him:

"The ladies are on their way to *Hinterindien.*"

I wince. Thousands of miles we have come to meet him, after a wait of two and a half years, and this is the first thing he is told, as if we were children. Julia starts to giggle with embarrassment. I cannot even open my mouth.

"Yes, yes," says Schweitzer. "Go right on and come to my room later." His eyes are incredibly kind. As he leaves, he smiles encouragingly.

Years later, I could laugh. But at that moment, the undignified first encounter was far from funny to me.

4

I KNOCK TIMIDLY at the door of Dr. Schweitzer's living quarters—a low one-story building, with a few steps leading to a porch.

"Come on in!" Schweitzer calls from inside. "No need to knock. The door is always open."

He motions us to sit down opposite his huge table which serves as a desk. It is covered with manuscripts, documents, and books. A yellow kitten is playing with a ball of string.

I take a deep breath and start speaking in German:

"Dr. Schweitzer, allow me to thank you for letting us come. We don't want to give you any trouble—"

"So. You don't want to give me any trouble, do you?" he interrupts. "No trouble, no inconvenience, indeed! Because of your kind consideration you failed to let me know the date of your arrival. Consequently, I've had to send a canoe to meet you every day for the past week. That means six men taken off their regular work! Don't you realize how much simpler it is if one knows what to expect? Your so-called civilization only complicates matters. When you come to the jungle, leave your polite manners at home!"

His voice by now booms like thunder, but I am not scared, for his eyes, in contrast to his voice, betray great gentleness, and there is a twinkle in them.

"This is your first lesson," he says, "and an important one: be natural and direct—act simply."

"I thought . . ." I stammer.

"Lesson number two—don't think," he goes on with a laugh. "Nothing much can come of it . . . just act out simply what you feel."

I nod, but dare not speak.

"Now that I have intimidated you thoroughly," he concludes, "I'll give you a little respite. Come down with me to the river.

This is the hour when I give Parsifal, Lohengrin, and Tristan *their* daily lessons."

Bewildered, Julia and I follow Dr. Schweitzer to the river. Three young pelicans greet him with a flutter of wings and waddle excitedly around him. A little native boy brings a pot full of fish.

"These pelicans were brought to the hospital with their wings clipped," explained the Doctor. "Now I must teach them how to fly and catch fish for themselves—quite an order for an old man like me!"

He picks out a small fish and pushes it gently into the eager mouth of a pelican.

"And now to work, Parsifal!" he exclaims. While he throws another fish into the water, he shoos Parsifal after it. "There! That's the way to catch fish," he calls out. "You'll learn."

He seems completely absorbed, and only after repeating the procedure with each of the birds, he turns to me and asks:

"So. Now tell me why you brought along all the camera equipment."

I try to explain that I've been asked to shoot a film on African sculpture.

"Ah, I see," he says. "So you don't plan an assault on me, too, by any chance?" He looks at me and through me.

"The real purpose of my trip, Dr. Schweitzer . . ." I start.

"Oh, no," he says. "All that was settled once and for all in my letter to you. No more of that."

"But Dr. Schweitzer . . ." I go on timidly. But he won't let me finish.

"Where did you say you were born?" he asks.

"Vienna," I tell him, almost relieved at the change of subject.

"Vienna. Yes, yes. Vienna," he repeats. "The time of the 'congress dances.' How different the world was in those days! The diplomats then were criticized for spending most of their time dancing—but they did help solve serious problems. Nowadays, when world leaders meet, one almost wishes they would dance; some dancing might do more good than all that talking which leads nowhere."

"Yes," I venture. "If people would only live up to their ideas, as you do—"

19 ह౿

But again he cuts me short with an impatient gesture.

"Understand one thing from the start!" he exclaims. "I don't like being put on a pedestal one bit, you hear? Stop it or we'll have no basis on which to be friends. That's lesson number three. Three lessons a day! At that rate we'll make your trip worth while, even if you can't take pictures."

I am crushed and dare not answer. I only make an attempt to smile. The sun is setting over the river, and the pelicans struggle back to the land. There is a silence, and I finally murmur:

"It's like a dream for me to be here at this hospital where you have worked for so many years, where you have helped so many people . . ."

Dr. Schweitzer lets his eyes wander over the hospital grounds.

"I was just lucky," he says. "Today I could never get the start I had then. Not just because of my age, but because the world has changed. When I came to Africa, you didn't even need a passport. Nowadays there's so much red tape, so much mistrust. When I was young, my friends thought me foolish, but they trusted my motives and helped me anyway . . . And then there was my stubbornness, my thick elephant's skin. That will be lesson number four. But not for today or even tomorrow. You know what I mean, don't you? You must not be hurt if your wishes don't come true . . ."

I know what he means all right. But I *am* hurt. You can't grow elephant's skin in a few minutes.

"Hey, Lohengrin! Parsifal! Tristan! Time to go home!" he shouts. And behind him the company falls into step, first the three pelicans, then myself, and Julia bringing up the rear.

We arrive at his porch. The three pelicans follow him to the steps, where a pregnant goat leaps to attention. As the Doctor opens his door, two dogs and the yellow kitten scurry in past him.

Julia, who had not understood our conversation in German, looks up at me expectantly:

"How did it go?"

"I have cut no ice with him, Julia," I confess. "He is dead set against the filming. There are too many things on his mind. I'll never convince him."

"Well at least we won't have to unpack then," says Julia, helpfully.

5

IT IS ALREADY DARK—night falls swiftly with only the briefest of twilights in the tropics—when Ali Silver, the young Dutch nurse, comes to guide us with her lantern to the dining hall. She shows us how to light our own kerosene lamps which we must carry with us.

"In Africa, always close the door quickly because of the insects," she advises us. "And make sure no snake is trailing you."

She leads the way under the mango and palm trees. Like glow-worms in the dark, the staff members, each carrying a lamp, converge on the big hall. Each lamp is labeled with a house and room number; ours reads *Sans Souci,* No. 5. As we put it down, alongside the others, we have the comfortable feeling that we are no longer strangers—that we belong.

Miss Silver introduces us to some thirty people gathered around the long table in the center of the room. They welcome us with much warmth, and the light from the kerosene lamps gives the room a festive but cozy glow. Dr. Schweitzer enters, hangs his brown, battered felt hat on a nail above the piano, and everyone sits down. Julia and I sit facing the Doctor, which is customary for new guests, we are told.

Dr. Schweitzer says a short prayer: "Thank the Lord for He is gentle, and His kindness is everlasting." The food is put on the table: steaming hot soup, some vegetables and fruit which are quite unfamiliar to me. Julia and I follow the example of the others by reaching out for second and third helpings. When one of the staff members wants to serve me, Dr. Schweitzer reprimands him.

"What is this?" he says. "Has the American influence undermined your Lambaréné morale? Everybody should look after himself in such trifling matters. She can serve herself perfectly well. It makes such a dreary commotion if everyone is continually asking each other 'A little more of this? A little more of that? Is everything all right?' No. No. Any civilized conversation is impossible with all that going on, so serve yourself well, and let the next fellow look to himself."

I agree with him, but keep quiet. If I uttered my agreement, he would surely poke fun at me and say: "Oh, you are still so polite you don't dare disagree with me."

There's a sense of peace at the table. The blue and gray jugs of Alsatian earthenware, in the light of the lamps, accentuate the tranquillity on the faces of the staff members, Dr. Schweitzer in their midst.

After the meal hymnbooks are handed out. They are worn but neatly held together with tape and string. Dr. Schweitzer begins to play on the old piano. It has an out-of-tune nickelodeon sound and some keys are stuck so that he sometimes has to skip a note, but it has great charm, and everyone joins in the singing. Returning to the table, he reads to us a short passage from the Scriptures, then gives an interpretation. The biblical people and places, the meaning of the ancient and familiar verses, come vividly to life for each of us around the table as Schweitzer speaks, for we are all aware of his lifetime of study and total commitment.

Afterward he says, "It's time I got back to work," and, nodding, turns toward Julia and me. "Sleep well your first night in Lambaréné!" We leave the dining room right after him, my eyes following him across the courtyard until I see him light the lamp in his room.

6

THE PROFOUND EXCITEMENT of my first day in Lambaréné keeps me awake for hours. While Julia snores
peacefully, I become increasingly tense and nervous, worrying
that my film project will never materialize. I even wonder if I'll
have another chance to talk quietly and alone with Dr. Schweitzer.

The night is a mélange of unfamiliar noises. Tom-toms drum
in the distance, chickens and ducks chatter in their sleep . . . Above
the croaking of frogs, the chirping of cicadas, and the screeching
of owls, I can hear the clanking of overripe mangoes falling on
tin roofs . . . And all night long birds and animals—their sounds
are so strange to me I never know which—keep up a lusty chatter.
I scarcely sleep at all.

At six-thirty when the first hospital bell rings, I get up grudg-
ingly, cross with myself, the world, and especially with Julia who
has slept like a log and is feeling irritatingly chipper. But after I
dress, my nerves quiet down, and Julia and I walk down to the
river. The mists are just rising and reveal the blue outlines of the
hills across the Ogowe. The sun glitters on the water, and many
of the native women are washing their laundry while their babies,
bundled securely to their mothers' backs, are still asleep.

Farther down at the landing, pirogues come in with new patients. Some look very sick and emaciated, and have to be carried
up to the hospital on stretchers. But even those in obvious pain
seem ready to return the smile and greeting of a stranger. The
compound starts to bustle with activity. Women prepare food
in iron cooking pots over small fires. Patients line up in long
rows in front of the hospital building to receive drugs and
treatment.

Mlle. Emma comes out of the maternity ward.

"Come along with me," she suggests. "I'll take time out to show
you around."

But just then the ringing of the bell calls us to the dining room.

At breakfast we sit again directly opposite Dr. Schweitzer. This time it's his sun helmet which he hangs above the piano. He nods at us with a friendly smile.

"You probably expect me to ask how you slept last night," he begins. "But I won't . . . I gave that up long ago. If you ask such questions, you get interminable answers: 'Oh, I was still awake at three in the morning, Docteur. At four I heard a frog croak, at five an owl screech,' and so on. No, better to get used to the idea that nobody really cares how you slept here in Lambaréné." And he laughs.

For breakfast there's a choice of coffee, tea, or cocoa, with delicious homemade white bread or toast and a variety of jams and marmalades made from tropical fruits. Butter has to be imported from Denmark or the Netherlands and is served twice a week only, on Thursdays and Sundays . . .

Mlle. Emma keeps her word and, after breakfast, takes us through the hospital building. The path from the landing leads straight to the long, low building, painted white and roofed with corrugated iron. The red color of the roof contrasts with the green of the umbrella tree which spreads out over the entire ward.

The hospital street is jammed with patients of all ages, awaiting their turn to be examined. Boys and girls carry paper tags on string around their necks, which record each individual name, time of arrival, and treatment given. The women, some young, others extremely old-looking, clad in their native togas or in tattered western dresses, chatter together. Men, some leaning on tall staffs, some supported by crutches, stand waiting, waiting . . .

That first day in Lambaréné I am overcome by the press of sick people with their swollen bodies, tumors, and open sores. Boussugou, Efaghe, Zambaboubamba, Camille—people I would meet and make friends with, whose specific sufferings and cures I would know in detail later on—are just a sequence of figures prostrate with fever or hunched in pain. Many of them have had to travel hundreds of miles to have a crippling illness treated, and I want to photograph them for those of us who can see a doctor any time a minor ailment troubles us.

We reach the postoperative ward just as Dr. Schweitzer is making the rounds with two assistants. One, Emma tells us, is Dr. Percy, a Hungarian refugee, who is in Lambaréné with his young

It is the baby antelope Jean-Baptiste who helps me get my first portrait of Dr. Schweitzer.

The path from the river-landing to the main hospital building at
Lambaréné is crowded with patients and workmen.

Most of my first pictures of Dr. Schweitzer were taken when he wasn't looking—for even though he had now given me permission to photograph him, I did not dare to face him. Below, Julia Knowlton, my assistant, holds the first batch of films ready to be mailed to New York for developing.

The "Grand Docteur" passes a line of patients waiting in the hospital street to receive their medicines at the clinic.

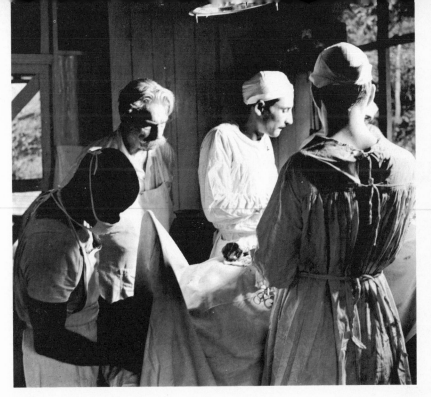

Dr. Schweitzer observes an operation performed by Dr. Emeric Percy. An orderly speaks quiet words of reassurance to the patient throughout the operation, since only a local anesthesia is required.

Midwife Devika Frankenbach proudly shows off the newest arrivals born at the hospital. Because of Schweitzer's efforts through the years in helping to overcome tribal taboos against twins, these two boys have been happily accepted by their parents.

The money awarded to Dr. Schweitzer through the Nobel Peace Prize of 1952 enabled him to replace leaf-shingle roofs, such as those above, with corrugated iron, in the leper village (right).

Dr. Schweitzer's day is varied and full. Above, left, he answers correspondence; below, left, he rehearses a Bach fugue; above, he takes advantage of a rest period during a busy day to converse with his workmen. His great vitality is in part due to his ability to move without pause from one activity to another.

Every Sunday morning, the bell is rung for worship. These scenes show services held in the hospital street: top left, Emma Hausknecht preaches a sermon in French as her words are translated into tribal tongues; above, Dr. Schweitzer and his patients attend another service.

Every day Schweitzer is the first one up, the last to bed. He is untiringly at work.

The moment Schweitzer is out of his room, animals come swarming to him from every direction.

wife. The other, Dr. Nägali, is an Alsatian who came to Africa right after finishing his studies at Strasbourg; he and his wife were married by Dr. Schweitzer in Lambaréné.

On seeing us with Mlle. Emma, Schweitzer says to her:

"You can go about your work, and leave them with me. That way you won't be held up."

Schweitzer concentrates completely on his work. He does not talk with Julia or me. Every patient knows and responds to him, as he pats their heads or exchanges jokes and small talk with them. There are many cases of hernia in this ward, of skin diseases, malaria, and tetanus. Some are the victims of attacks by wild animals. Though many of the dark faces look feverish, all look grateful. We move on to the urological ward, and then into the *pouponnière*—the babies' ward. A young Swiss nurse holds up a tiny infant to Dr. Schweitzer.

"This is my screamer," she says. "I don't know what to do. I took him to my room last night—he was so weak I was very worried. When I hold him, he is quiet and contented. But the moment I turn away, he starts screaming with all his might. Still, there seems nothing wrong with him."

"Let him scream," Dr. Schweitzer tells her. "He's all right. He is just finding out what a good heart you have." He slaps the little tot on his bare behind and walks through the passage underneath the maternity ward, toward the river.

At eleven o'clock a horn blows.

"Ration time," explains Dr. Schweitzer. "The patients are lining up for their food. You can watch. In fact, if you're good, you may get a banana yourself by lining up with the others! I must go back to my room and attend to some letters."

I watch him walk up the hill toward his house. He seems tired now, but so am I, and so are the two young doctors after their rounds. The heat is excessive.

"Does he come to the wards every day?" I ask.

"I don't think he's ever missed a day," says Dr. Nägeli. "His will power is tremendous; sometimes I think he does everything out of sheer Alsatian stubbornness."

About three hundred people—patients and their relatives—are standing in line before an open window of the hut where Mrs. Percy dispenses the rations. Each patient has a tag, on which she

41 ॐ

marks what each has received, so that no one can come around a second time! The patients are allowed to bring their families. Those in good health pay for their treatment with some kind of work or service. The women clear the jungle, wash the hospital linen, or work in the garden. The men help on construction or general repair work.

The bell calls us to lunch. Bell is not quite the right word, for it consists of two strips of old railroad track which hang from a pole and are struck with a metal bar. Mealtime means more to me than just the nourishment of the body. It is such a good opportunity to watch Dr. Schweitzer and listen to his conversations. A photographer could not pray for a more colorful subject than this man as he goes about his work. He does everything with directness and simplicity—administering the hospital, seeing to his correspondence, ordering drugs and instruments, or looking after the animals. But I have not mentioned the film again . . . I have not even the courage to write Jerome Hill yet. I just hope we'll be allowed to stay a week or two longer, and then I will go to the Cameroon to film some native woodcarvings, or perhaps join the safari organized by the hunter from Columbus, Ohio!

My heart is heavy as I think of the parting.

7

AFTER LUNCH Schweitzer leaves the dining room, his pockets crammed with bread crusts and leftovers. I follow him out because I want to ask him if I can at least take some snapshots.

The moment Schweitzer is out of the door, animals and birds come swarming to him from every direction—cats, dogs, chickens, goats, and ducks. Three little chimpanzees stumble over one another, trying to get there first. After feeding them generously, the Doctor walks to the antelope cage, still pursued by the whole menagerie. Four beautiful antelopes approach him and nuzzle into his pockets.

"What pictures I could take!" I cannot help exclaiming.

"This is Jean-Baptiste," says Schweitzer, picking up the youngest one. "He is named after Johann Sebastian Bach."

"May I get my still camera and take *one* shot?" I beg.

"Well, just for a memento," he says. "But don't get any ideas about putting me in the picture."

Before he can finish the sentence, I am off. Back in my room, I grab the Rolleiflex from under the bed and rush back. Jean-Baptiste looks at me with the eyes of an innocent and curious child. As I observe Dr. Schweitzer, surrounded by the antelopes, I think: "How much his eyes resemble theirs." When I mention it, he laughs it off, scoldingly.

"You're trying to prey on my vanity," he says. "Flattery will get you no place. But if you want to photograph the animals, go ahead. You seem much happier with a camera in your hands."

I start shooting through the fence.

"No, no. Come in here," says Schweitzer. "I will hold him up for you." And of course I make quite sure that the Doctor gets into the picture.

And so it is the baby antelope Jean-Baptiste who helps me get my first portrait of Dr. Schweitzer. After that, I trail the Doctor diligently and try to get other snapshots of him, but all I can ever catch is a view of his back. I cannot muster up the courage again to face him head-on with my camera.

For two weeks I watch Dr. Schweitzer in his daily contacts with the staff and his patients. It seems that he, whose judgment rests on reason and common sense, more often than not lets his heart rule his mind. Sometimes I hear the Doctor say to a man who has been unusually lazy on his job: "Don't bother to come for your ration tonight. You don't deserve it, and you won't get it." But invariably the man does receive his food.

One day a patient who has been dismissed as cured breaks into the pharmacy and steals some drugs. Schweitzer does not tell the police. He merely tells the thief in no uncertain terms never to return to the hospital settlement again. And yet, when the man later comes back sick, he is of course given treatment.

Eventually I have to ask myself: Is making a movie important enough to warrant the heavy involvement of a man whose every day is dedicated to selfless work for others? By comparison, my own wishes are merely inspired by selfish ambition. No—better to renounce my project and let Dr. Schweitzer work in peace!

Once I have reached this conclusion, I ask Mlle. Emma to arrange for our departure.

Several days later, as I am wandering about the hospital grounds with sadness in my heart, I stop in front of the antelopes' cage, right across from Dr. Schweitzer's window.

"I want to show you something." It is Schweitzer's voice at his window. I run up the steps but hesitate at his door. He is sitting at the table, writing.

"Come in, don't be so shy. But softly; don't waken her." He points at the little cat all rolled up on a bundle of letters. I tiptoe nearer to him.

"Look how relaxed and at ease she is," he says, turning toward me. "How about you? Do you feel as much at home here too?"

"Yes," I reply. "I like it so much that I am prepared to leave without pestering you any more about the film."

He looks up at me in surprise and asks:

"But you would be happier, wouldn't you, if you could go home with material for a film?"

"Of course," I reply. "But I see it all a bit differently now. I think I understand why you refuse."

Schweitzer looks at me, a twinkle in his eye.

"Listen," he says. "I have been thinking over your request. In a short time you have become one of us. Somehow I cannot let you go home without fulfilling your heart's desire. I will give you permission to gather material. We will work on the film together. But on one condition: You must not worry about a release date. The film should be shown only after my death as a memory to my friends."

There is a pause, for I am unable to say a word. Then Schweitzer continues:

"Go on now. Tomorrow the sun will be shining. I can tell. I'm a bit of a peasant, you know, who can forecast the weather. So to your work with joy, and I'll help you as much as I can. But don't tell anyone except the gentleman who sent you. Otherwise, I'll be besieged by protests. One more thing—your first name. What is it?"

"Erica."

"Erica," he repeats. "Why didn't you tell me right way? *Erikas* —the small wildflowers—were my mother's favorite. They used to remind her of the high mountains around the Münster Valley where she came from. All her life she longed to go back there. Maybe one day we will visit there if you ever come to Günsbach."

I run back to my room in a trance.

"Julia, Julia!" I call out. "He understands! He has given us permission to start filming tomorrow! Can you believe it? Shall I be worthy of his trust?"

"Probably not," says Julia, shaking her head. "It only goes to show Dr. Schweitzer's magnanimity! Well, what are you waiting for? Let's get the cameras out from under the beds!"

We crouch on the floor and extricate the camera cases, which are covered with a rich growth of tropical fungus.

8

AT BREAKFAST Schweitzer nods at me and says:
"I've arranged for someone to help carry your cameras. He's ten years old, and his name is Zambaboubamba. His father is a patient here, and the boy's offered to help out. He's not very big, but his intentions are good."

When we leave the dining room, Zambaboubamba is sitting on the front steps, waiting. Schweitzer introduces us.

"At this age they are still eager to work," Schweitzer says. "Later on, some become too lazy even to yawn."

Zambaboubamba is very proud when I hand him the camera case. (I carefully hang on to the camera myself.) Gingerly he balances it on his head and offers both hands to carry more. But I persuade him to hold the case with both hands. Julia and I carry the tripods and extra film.

I want first to film hospital activities which do not involve Schweitzer directly; I can concentrate on him later, when he's used to seeing the cameras around and has more confidence in me. I set up my equipment in the courtyard in front of Schweitzer's house, where much work goes on. Several natives are making mats; others sit at old-fashioned Singer sewing machines, making "boo-boos," which are shirts and short pants for the native helpers. Opposite Schweitzer's room and across the yard is the kitchen building where a small market is in full swing. While we are getting set up, one of the nurses who has been skeptical about the film from the start comes by. She is not won over yet.

"If I go to heaven," she says, "it will be because I try to protect our Docteur from interruptions of his work."

"But please, *Mademoiselle*," I reply. "I am already in heaven, in seventh heaven, because the Docteur has given me permission to take pictures. Believe me, I will try not to bother him."

Just then Schweitzer comes along, and she repeats to him what I said.

"I just couldn't let her leave without pictures," he explains. "She looked too sad." And Schweitzer goes trudging off.

We walk down to the river, Zambaboubamba ahead of us. He is envied by the other boys his age and walks very proudly and solemnly, looking neither right nor left. I'm still afraid that the camera case will go toppling off his head any minute, but, like all the natives, he's been balancing heavy weights on his head since he learned to walk. It is partly this training that makes their posture and movement so straight and free. We photograph the river and the arrival of pirogues with patients. Schweitzer appears again. I'm still terrified to point my camera at him, and stop shooting.

A motor launch draws up at the landing, and a man climbs out. Schweitzer rushes toward him with outstretched hands. A few moments later we are introduced—he as M. Perron, one of Schweitzer's close friends, and I as a "new addition to the hospital."

I use the incident to make my first film of Schweitzer as he walks up the hill with his friend. It is from the rear, as nearly all my first shots of him prove to be. I still don't have the courage to tackle him head-on.

Black storm clouds are gathering, and Julia and I walk back to our room with its two beds, the washstand, and the simple bare table. I sit down at my typewriter and write a few letters home. Unfortunately, the walls are so thin that the typewriter can be heard throughout *Sans Souci,* and only during a rainstorm is the racket drowned out.

By lunchtime Julia and I are ravenous. The main course is crocodile meat, called *chima,* breadfruit, and tomato and cucumber salad. Breadfruit tastes like potatoes and is an excellent substitute for them. Potatoes can't be grown in Africa because the stems shoot up so fast that the potato root itself has no time to develop. Cucumbers are different from ours—smaller, slightly bitter, but very tasty. In fact, all the vegetables are good, despite the fact that they are washed with a disinfectant to guard against dysentery. Only natural fertilizer is used in the soil in Lambaréné—a major function of the two hundred and fifty goats and sheep at the hospital. As for the crocodile meat, I politely decline, not feeling quite up to that yet. I stuff myself, though, on the tropical fruit salad, which is delicious: a generous mixture of papayas, guavas, oranges, grapefruit, mangoes, and *pommes de cythère*, which taste like the best applesauce. The water is served from the beautiful Alsatian jugs. It is thoroughly boiled and filtered, and flavored with the juice of a lime.

When I comment on the quality of the fruit, Schweitzer says it is quite a job to plant and raise fruit trees and vegetables, especially during the dry season.

"On top of that," he says, "the indigènes never think of the future. In their impatience, they often cut into the young fruit and ruin it before it's ripe."

When he asks me if I eat as well in New York as in Lambaréné, I tell him that at home I usually cook my meals from cans. He throws up his arms.

"Typical," he says. "Women are not proud of their art in cooking any more. In fact, they've practically forgotten how to cook at all. I remember a lady from Munich who was once very wealthy. But she lost all her money, and could only afford to rent a small room without any kitchen. She told me, 'I would be so happy if only I could cook again.' Unfortunately, so often one must lose everything to become aware of one's privileges."

I explain to him how little time working girls like me have for preparing food and that it's very practical to be able to fall back on canned food. But he insists that canned food is not so healthful as fresh.

In the afternoon we have permission from Dr. Schweitzer's assistants, Dr. Percy and Dr. Nägeli, to film in the operating room. The first operation scheduled is the removal of a fibroid tumor. I've never seen an operation before, and am a little afraid. Dr. Percy explains the procedure to me. The patient, a woman, is given a spinal anaesthetic—ether is hard to use because it evaporates quickly in the heat. She seems quite free of fear, and even laughs a little with the native orderly who stands at her head and softly whispers into her ear. The light above the operating table is weak; but Dr. Percy operates calmly and skillfully. There is no sound in the room. Standing just a few feet away on a large stool, I see everything—the removal of the tumor and the sewing up of the incision. The patient, a bit dazed, is wheeled out to her waiting family, who will stay with her in the ward.

The next operation is an emergency—a Caesarean section on a very young woman. There is great danger that the child will be stillborn. The girl herself is in great pain. Her crying is so rhythmic and melodious it sounds like a soft chant. A nurse breathes for half an hour into the mouth of the tiny child, all the while tapping it gently on the back, and the little boy lives!

Dr. Schweitzer tells me that Caesareans are now very frequent in Lambaréné. "It was quite a different matter when I first came," he says. "In 1913 the old women of the village all acted as midwives. Men were not even permitted to go outdoors when a birth was in progress. They were so scared of the old ladies they would never have dared to anyway. But many women were dying in childbirth. The elders would advise the young women never to see a doctor—that it would bring bad luck. How can I gain power over these old witches? I thought. Nothing I said made any difference. Then I hit on the idea to present each baby born at my hospital with a little bonnet and dress. And the people reacted, 'If the doctor gives out a bonnet and dress for each child, for quite ordinary children, surely something good and special must come of it.' So you see, by sheer bribery, my power was established, and pregnant women have flocked to the hospital ever since!"

Later in the evening, on the way to *Hinterindien*, I pass the Doctor's room and hear him playing the piano with pedal attachments. It is strange to hear Bach in the jungle, above the rustling of the mango trees and the whistling of birds in the palms. It sounds so beautiful that I keep standing there for a long while, below his room, listening.

9

AFTER BREAKFAST TODAY Dr. Schweitzer offers to accompany Julia and me to the leper village, which is just a ten-minute walk from the hospital.

"Put on strong shoes," he says, glancing suspiciously at our white sandals. "Or don't you have proper footwear with you? The lepers walk through the grass, and many of them have open sores. You might cut your legs on the sharp-edged grass, and any open wound becomes easily infected. Have you not noticed the sandals my patients wear? They are made here by our hospital shoemaker. He sits on my veranda, where we can keep an eye on him. He cuts them out from discarded automobile tires. I'll be ready to go with you at ten. Pick me up in my room, yes? But on one condition. Don't take your cameras yet. It's better if they first get used to you without them."

He is probably quite right, and I am intrigued that the Doctor is assuming the role of "director." While waiting for him, we take a few shots of people lining up for their daily rations. They carry either tin cans or large leaves in which they place their bananas and rice. I am beginning to distinguish individual faces, and a friendly grin here and there shows that some of them also recognize me. Already they are less reluctant to be filmed, but many still run off from my camera, screaming in French: "Don't take my face! Don't take my face!" This stems from the superstition that in having one's picture taken one has one's "soul" taken away, too. As if a photographer in Africa did not have enough problems already!

By ten o'clock I have lost track of Julia, and head for Dr. Schweitzer's room; I see him at his desk, concentrating on some papers he holds in his hands. I hesitate to disturb him, but, without looking up, he murmurs:

"Shy again? Come in! Come in! And I shall be with you shortly."

I sit down opposite his desk. Only a wire netting separates his room from the outside. I feel a deep sense of tranquillity, as if Schweitzer's calm concentration had the power of putting all things in perspective. He seems to have forgotten my presence completely. He writes a few sentences, then turns his face toward the window, letting his eyes rove over the river, the palm trees, and the jungle in front of his African home. How often he must have sat here with his thoughts on his writing or his music—precious hours stolen from his work at the hospital. I am but one more interruption. Just as I turn away from him, heavy with guilt, he looks up and says:

"*Allons! Allons!* It is high time we were off! And don't feel badly that you take me from my desk."

"Are you clairvoyant?" I ask. "I was just about to go."

"Your thoughts are not hard to read," he says with a laugh. "They are clearly written on your face. Come! The walk will be good. We'll go up through the plantation and back by the road along the river."

The small road that we follow climbs quite sharply. I breathe more rapidly, but Dr. Schweitzer never stops talking. He points with the pride of a farmer to the various fruit trees that surround us.

"Don't think they just grow up on their own," he says. "To start with, I had to plant over a thousand fruit trees. The jungle overgrows everything so fast you have to weed, cut back, tend the trees constantly. During the dry season we have to fetch water from the river in buckets. Otherwise many of these trees would die. I want always to have enough fruit in Lambaréné so that my patients may take what they please without being accused of stealing. I want this plantation to be the closest thing to the Garden of Eden—a paradise!"

He laughs and plucks a yellow star-shaped fruit off a tree.

"Have you ever tried a carambole?"

I never have. He takes a knife from his baggy trousers pocket and cuts the fruit open.

"Here," he says, handing me a piece. "Let's share it. Ripened and warmed in the sun. It tastes better than any fruit stored in a refrigerator. Isn't that true? It brings out the true taste. *Bon appetit!*"

The fruit is delicious, unlike anything I've tasted before. As we share the carambole, Julia comes rushing up the hill, all puffing and red in the face.

"I've looked for you everywhere!" she exclaims. "Oh, that heat. I could hardly make it up here."

"Never run in the heat of the sun," says Dr. Schweitzer, shaking his finger at her. "That's one rule that all my helpers are happy to follow. Always walk like a dignified lady out for a Sunday stroll. Now wipe off your face, and join us on the grand tour."

He hands Julia a huge clean handkerchief.

When we reach the leper village, men and women welcome him, exclaiming, *"Bolo, Bolani . . .* Hello, Doctor!" We stop often as Dr. Schweitzer talks to them. But I am silent with horror at so much suffering, so many cripples. The huts are small, and I have to stoop to enter. None of them has any furniture, only mats on the ground, or ramshackle bunks. And these tiny cubicles are draped with dirty clothing; chickens and children run in and out, while the sick lie crowded together on the earthen floor.

Schweitzer explains some of the problems that arise in treating the lepers.

"Sometimes the chief of a village will arrive here, with six of his wives," he says. "Though only one wife may be ill, it's impossible to make them understand that she should live apart lest the others become infected. This insistence that whole families must live together here, though only one member may be afflicted, is the reason that everything's so overcrowded, both here in the leper village and in the wards of the hospital. But one cannot change their ways easily. If they weren't assured that they could stay together here, they would not come at all. I must treat them on their own terms or not at all. That is what many who are critical of the conditions here do not understand.

"Fortunately," he continues, "leprosy is not as contagious as we used to think. But continued treatment is made difficult by the reluctance of the patients to remain here unless they're in pain. Leprosy, you see, is a disease of the nerve ends. The danger lies in this very insensitivity. It seems foolish to them to stay here getting stuck with needles and swallowing pills, once the pain's stopped. They go back to their villages, and return to the hospital only when they're in agony. But by that time it may be too late, and little can be done for them. It's a continuous struggle to make them stay until their state is arrested. Even that can take a year or two. I have to humor them, which takes time, or shout and punish them if humoring does no good."

As we go through the village, Schweitzer points out that most of the huts are in bad condition.

"A whole new village must be built here," he says. "And I must get started soon. There is little use in doing patchwork, here and there. But when and with what money can I do it? I often feel like a kind of beggar on borrowed time. But one thing I know. Once I start it, it will be finished. It has always been that way in my life."

He takes us to the top of a hill where giant jungle trees crowd against one another.

"It is here I must begin clearing the jungle," he says. "I have it all in my mind. I never used a blueprint or sketch. There will be several rows of neat houses, each with its own kitchen. They'll provide enough space for about two hundred and fifty patients and their families. I wish I could roof the houses with corrugated iron! The raffia we use now needs repairing every year. But I'll need lots of wood and time, and money and people to help me."

"Will you let me take pictures while you build?" I ask.

"So. You are just as optimistic as I am." He laughs. "And I see you have a share of the same stubbornness, too. Well, we'll see. Perhaps, as a price for taking your pictures, you will give me a hand with the actual work?"

"Indeed I would be happy to," I reply. "But I'd be a most unskilled laborer."

"Leave that problem to me." Schweitzer smiles. "I shall find you a suitable job; many jobs. I'm a past master at putting people to work. One says I'm a kind of tyrant. If I weren't I'd get nothing done, I think."

We return to the hospital in single file, Schweitzer leading the way through the forest. The shade is deep and cool, and it seems as if we were walking through a green cathedral, built of trees. Back at the landing, life is bustling with activity. From dozens of pirogues the natives are disembarking; the women in their colorful clothes have pots and pans and bundles strapped to their backs, and on their heads they carry cages bulging with squawking chickens.

The line waiting for rations looks enormous.

"They eat me poor," sighs Schweitzer, but a twinkle in his eye shows he takes it with his ever-ready humor. "The truth is that they hardly get enough. A shipment of rice is late. We have little left. I do hope it comes soon. From our visit to the leper village perhaps you'll have some idea of the 'prose' of my life."

I start to thank him, but he sees what is coming and raises his hand.

"No more thanks. Save your energy for your work. It is more profitable. You are on your own now. Go to the village anytime, and shoot to your heart's delight."

Some stretcher bearers are lifting a new patient out of a boat. Schweitzer leaves us and follows them up to the hospital.

10

ONE MORNING we get up very early and dress hurriedly in the darkness. Dr. Schweitzer has arranged for a motorboat to take us into Lambaréné so that I can mail some films back to New York. When we get into town, the post office is still closed, and we trudge through a heavy rain to the market place, where ramshackle stands are overloaded with small mirrors, pearl necklaces, and other cheap trinkets and bric-a-brac. By the time the post office opens we are soaked through, and it turns out that my packages of film are too heavy and must be completely re-packed. The large African stamps hardly fit onto the small packages, and I wonder whether the films will ever get to America. A mood of nagging depression comes over me, and I start to brood about the films themselves. I have so many shots of the hospital grounds, the natives, and all the animals, but so few of Dr. Schweitzer! One problem has been my own shyness in facing him with the camera; the other is the Doctor's habit of stiffening up when the camera is on him and assuming some kind of unnatural pose. He seems not to understand or approve of the "catch" or "candid" shot. Obviously, the only way to break this resistance down is to be around him so much that he takes no notice of my cameras. But how long will this take? Julia and I have made reservations to fly back in less than two weeks' time, and, I feel, for all hospitality, that we are becoming an imposition to Dr. Schweitzer and his staff. On the other hand, if my project turns out to be a failure now, it will be all the more inexcusable after winning Dr. Schweitzer's consent. By the time we board the motorboat again, I am feeling very sorry for myself, indeed.

As we ride back, the river water looks dull and angry in the morning drizzle, but the hospital grounds, once we pass the last bend in the river, look oddly welcoming. Perhaps it was merely homesickness I'd felt back in the town—homesickness for Schweitzer's Lambaréné that soon I will be leaving for good. I am suddenly so happy just to be back at the hospital that I forget all my worries about the film.

Waiting at the landing for me is my little assistant, Zambaboubamba. He's become much less shy during the past several days and repeatedly asks about America.

"I would like to stay with you all the time, all the rest of my life," he says. "Will you take me back with you to America?"

I ask him what has brought this on. "Aren't you happy here, Zamba?"

"The Grand Docteur makes us work too hard," he explains.

"Don't you enjoy your work?" I ask him.

"With you I do," he replies. "But it would be nicer just to rest and take it easy. Anyway, the Grand Docteur has lots of money. He doesn't need to make us work."

"Where did you hear that?" I asked.

"I listen to the grown-ups talking," he replies. They say he gets pots of money in Europe just for playing the organ."

"And then he spends it all on you," I tell him. "Don't you know this?"

"Oh, I like the Grand Docteur well enough," Zamba admits. "But I'd like him better if he gave us some money, too. We are so poor."

"Why, what would you do with money?" I ask him. "You don't have to buy cloth. When you're hungry, you get fish and rice and you can always go and pick fruit. When you don't feel well, the good doctors and nurses treat you with expensive medicines. We in Europe and America have to work very hard for all this, and we never get it for free."

"Just the same, Zamba wants to go with you to America," he replies, smiling, and dances around me, showing off his handmade necklace of burnt-out flash bulbs.

At lunchtime Schweitzer is in high spirits and hands me a fat envelope filled with stamps.

"Share them in sisterly fashion with your companion," he tells me. "They are stamps from all over the world, and quite valuable. If you sell them in New York perhaps you can get enough money to buy yourself a petticoat."

I accept gratefully.

"You know," Schweitzer continues, "letters addressed to me

sometimes don't get here. When they come from outlandish places, somebody somewhere along the line has found out that one can turn stamps into money. Don't forget to share! And, yes; this is important: Don't buy yourself cigarettes with the money raised. You smoke too much. You should give it up. The money you usually spend on cigarettes might pay for your next trip to Lambaréné."

"I will try," I reply. "But I am not sure that I have the necessary will power."

"I once smoked even more than you do," Schweitzer says. "It was terrible. I smoked heavily and I smoked everything I could get my hands on—cigars, cigarettes, and pipes. When I was studying at the university, I could not even put a thought down on paper without being swathed in a cloud of smoke. Eventually, I could not even get out of bed in the morning without having a smoke first. Then I said to myself, 'This thing has got out of hand.' I did not give it up, though, until the turn of the century. I was in Paris, and on the evening of the last day of the year 1899, I threw out my cigarettes and cigars. Then I cleaned my pipes, put them away, and promised myself never to draw another breath of smoke the rest of my life."

"Do you mean you haven't smoked since?" I ask.

"Of course not," he says, with a beautiful childlike naïve expression, as if it were the most natural, the only way.

"Well, what about the women right here at the hospital?" I ask. "I've seen several of them smoking pipes."

"That's quite all right," says Schweitzer. "They're old ladies. They're used to it, and they'd miss it badly if I interfered. Besides, they make their own tobacco from the leaves they pick. But the young people, I don't allow them to smoke. When I catch them with cigarettes, that they've bought, I make them stamp them out. Then I give them a lecture about copying the bad habits of Westerners. For all the good it does! It simply means that they seldom let me catch them at it. So it goes."

During lunch I ask Mlle. Emma whether I might take a few shots in the dining room, for I don't dare ask Dr. Schweitzer. But he overhears me and says:

"My, what a timid little bird is here with us. You really think I am a monster, eh?"

I shake my head.

"Well, the truth is that I don't like pictures of people eating," he says. "But perhaps we can arrange it for you later, some other time."

For dessert I'm amazed to have a dish I have not tasted for years. It's a kind of pastry called *Faschingskrapfen* that's well liked in Vienna, especially during carnival time.

"Your mother would be surprised that you eat these tartlets here in deep Africa, yes?" asks Schweitzer.

"Indeed she would be," I reply. "And to tell the truth, the ones I've had in Vienna were never as good as these."

"Serve yourself well," he urges. "And your companion, too. Because she speaks neither French nor German, she may be too shy to eat as much as she can."

I translate for Julia, who replies:

"Already, my dresses are becoming too small for me, and I anticipate leaving here in a sarong."

I pass on this information, and everybody smiles.

"Here," Schweitzer says, "you eat as much as you like without worrying about your figure. The tropical heat takes care of excess weight. You sweat enough and save yourself the trouble of going to a Turkish bath."

After lunch I watch Schweitzer standing amidst the antelopes, across from his house. He gives them scraps from the table and talks to them, naming each with a soft voice. They are as eager to lick his hands as to eat the bread. The scene would be perfect for my camera, and a renewed wave of impatience comes over me. Does Schweitzer really want me to stay and film, or is he hoping, deep down, that I'll go soon and leave him in peace? How I wish this question would stop tormenting me!

I watch him walk toward the river with his three pelicans, their cut wings flapping shyly.

"But you must be patient," I hear Schweitzer telling them. "First you learn to fish in the river. Later you can take off and watch us all from the air. A small step at a time—that's always the best way."

Is the Doctor really clairvoyant, I wonder? In any case, I resolve to follow his advice to the pelicans for the time being. Accordingly, I humbly devote all afternoon to photographing the animals of Lambaréné, and by dinnertime I am more composed. I must stop being such an eager beaver, I tell myself.

At the dinner table the atmosphere is quiet and conversation subdued. The Doctor seems out of sorts. He leans his head on his hands and speaks to no one. As soon as he's played the hymn and said the evening prayer, he abruptly gets up and leaves the dining room. I have never seen him like this before, and wonder what is the matter. Dr. Percy says that Schweitzer is probably concentrating on some problem, and merely does not want his thoughts disturbed. I get the premonition that it has something to do with me, with my presence in Lambaréné. Just then, Mlle. Emma comes over and tells me:

"Dr. Schweitzer wishes to see you in his room."

Nervously, I hurry there through the darkness, my kerosene light trembling in my hand. As I enter, he says:

"It is time you and I had a little talk."

This is it, I'm convinced. The kitten watches him from the washstand.

"My dear little kitten," he says to her. "Yes. Yes. That's what I call you in public. But when we are alone, I say you are a little red beast, right?"

The kitten stares at him, quizzically.

"Now," he begins again and turns to me, "what is this I hear about your having made reservations to fly back next week? You have committed a serious sin. You should have discussed this matter with me. You are in my care now. You are my guest, and I will tell you when I think you should leave. What is the matter with you? For months you hound me to make a film. You refuse to take no for an answer, but now that you have my permission you want to leave before you have even started. Is there something bothering you?"

"Dear Dr. Schweitzer," I start, "it's just that I feel . . . a burden . . . the film . . . it will take so much time . . . you are busy . . ."

"Once and for all, stop this nonsense," says Schweitzer, putting his hand over my mouth. "Have you forgotten what I told you? Do you think I do not mean what I say? Now listen. My grandfather used to say when he watched the building of organs, 'As long as people are allowed to work unhurriedly, in their own time, they will build great organs. Once they start fabricating organs to save time and labor, we shall lose the quality of those great masterpieces.' My grandfather was right, and you would do well to remember his words, too. Take all the time you need on this film. It must grow in its own way. Soon I'll be able to spend more hours with you, myself. Until then, carry your camera lightly. Stop, look, and listen. Stay, if you can, a few more weeks this trip. Then go. Acquire some perspective. See how your films have worked out technically, and come back soon. Make as many trips back as you wish. And what about the gentleman who is sending you, Mr. Jerome Hill? Perhaps he would like to come with you sometime? I would like him to see what he spends his good money for. There is just one condition. The one I mentioned before. When the film is finished, it must absolutely not be released before my death. If you accept that, we are in accord. Now I hope that your doubts are dispelled, once and for all."

I keep quiet, knowing how annoyed Schweitzer gets with any elaborate display of gratitude.

"Congratulations!" he tells me after a few moments. "I see that already you are learning the virtue of silence. There is hope for you yet. Have you noticed our shoemaker, the fellow who works on my veranda, cutting sandals from old tires? He is a mute. I always tell him that because he cannot talk he has the place of honor!"

While Schweitzer has been talking, Pierette, the red cat, has spied a plump bug near the kerosene light. Now she sits, transfixed, ready to jump.

"Hey there! Reverence for life!" calls Schweitzer. "Leave the poor creature in peace." And he affectionately swipes the kitten off the table.

I wish him good night and walk back to *Sans Souci*. A heavy burden has been lifted from my shoulders.

11

EARLY ONE AFTERNOON Julia and I make an expedition to a neighboring village with a Mr. Hug, a painter and a brother of the Swiss nurse who supervises the kitchen. We borrow some heavy boots, and, accompanied by Zamba, my little camera bearer, and a native guide, we go trudging off into the jungle. I feel very small and awed as we worm our way beneath the giant trees. Here and there specks of sunlight filter through the foliage onto ferns and wild flowers.

Suddenly, out of nowhere, a little boy joins us. Zamba tells me that he is from the neighboring village and that his name is Makulo. There is nothing he has to do, no one looking for him, and soon he volunteers to help me and Zamba with the cameras.

We cross little rivers, push our way through thick jungle, and both Julia and I feel as though we are on a dangerous expedition. But the closest thing to "wild animals" we encounter are dramatically colored birds, chirping happily. We see no snakes, no elephants, no lions, no tigers.

"Actually, the noise of the hospital is so great that it chases the wild animals away," Mr. Hug tells us. "Only a boa constrictor occasionally finds its way to the hospital. I was there once when they found one with six little pigs inside of her."

"I'm glad that was before our arrival." Julia remarks.

The jungle grass is so sharp that when kneeling down for a picture I cut myself.

"Take care. Put some iodine on it," Mr. Hug warns me. "In this heat wounds heal badly and have a tendency to fester."

By the time we arrive at the village we are really worn out, purple in the face and parched with thirst. Mr. Hug warns us not to touch any water outside of the hospital settlement, but when someone offers us a coconut, we cut it open and drink the milk.

Makulo wants to take us to the chief of the village. He is very proud because the chief is his father, and he wants to introduce us to him. The village is small, with some two hundred inhabitants, and its forty or fifty huts are built on a plateau. A ropemaker, sitting in front of his home, spinning rope, is quite willing to be photographed, but most of the women, including several real beauties, run away in spite of Makulo's rapid explanations that we are friends of the Grand Docteur and can do as we please.

The biggest hut in the village belongs to the chief. He has an imposing figure. He bows slightly to us, and his handshake is so powerful that I have to massage my hand afterward to loosen it up. His face resembles a huge gorilla's and looks quite fierce. But his manner is gentle and amiable. He has four wives who obviously live in great harmony with one another. Three of them have babies tagging after them; the fourth one, Makulo's mother, is busy cooking. The chief tells me that there is strict division of work, one wife doing the laundry, the other looking after the plantation, the third selling the fruit and other produce, and the fourth handling the housework.

"Don't they ever fight and get jealous of each other?" I ask.

"Why should they?" he replies, surprised at the question. "After I have a baby with one I must not touch her until the child is weaned. That sometimes takes three years, so naturally I have to marry another. That's our custom. But it's very expensive these days. I have to pay anywhere from fifty to two hundred dollars for a wife, depending upon her quality. It's too much. And if I don't pay up in full, the family of my wife comes and takes her away." He looks around and sighs, "Oh yes, life is hard in the jungle of Africa."

On the way back we stop at the small mission station where Dr. Schweitzer started his African career. The house that he and Mrs. Schweitzer lived in is still standing, but terribly dilapidated. At the mission station we are greeted by a French missionary, who invites us to have tea with him. About two hundred pupils who go to school there are just leaving their classes, and we watch some of them crowding into the boats which will take them back to the Lambaréné hospital. It is pleasant to sit on the veranda, to sip tea and listen to this gentle man, who is greatly concerned about saving the old Schweitzer house.

"It is a landmark," he says. "It should not be allowed to rot and disintegrate. When you return to the States, perhaps you could help me raise funds to preserve it."

I promise to do what I can.

By boat we go back to the hospital, arriving just in time for dinner. Schweitzer is working on a speech he's promised to give over the Brazzaville radio. "My trouble is," he explains, "that I do not like to speak extemporaneously. Or just from notes. I have to write the whole thing out in longhand, and then memorize it. The writing should be finished tonight."

After breakfast next morning I'm taking a short stroll when I notice a great commotion in front of Schweitzer's house. A group of natives are carrying an animal on poles between them. The animal turns out to be a wild pig, and "wild" is right. Though its legs are bound with ropes, it moves in such fear and with such force that the natives can hardly hold it. Schweitzer rushes out to learn what's going on.

"We found him in the jungle, Grand Docteur," a native tells him. "In a trap. There is something wrong with left hind leg."

"Let's see, but don't unbind him," Schweitzer says. "I will do it. I'm afraid that when he is unbound he will hurt you. Let's carry him behind the kitchen."

Off they march with the frightened animal. I follow with my camera. Behind the kitchen is a large enclosure where Schweitzer and the natives put the animal down.

"Now everybody leave," Schweitzer commands.

The natives seem glad to obey his order and retreat quickly behind the wire netting. I am terrified that the animal is going to hurt Schweitzer. Carefully, the Doctor loosens the ropes and talks incessantly with a soft voice:

"Don't be afraid. Your troubles are over. Come now. Be a good fellow."

I want to enter the enclosure to get a shot of Schweitzer bending over the pig, but he shouts at me:

"Away with you, at once!"

So I retreat, too, and watch him from the outside. As if he were sorry for shouting, he calls me over when he's finished untying the ropes.

"I will call him Jonas. That's a good name for him, isn't it?"

Jonas escapes into the opposite corner from Schweitzer. He is running around, limping and leaping like a bucking horse.

"Get water, palm nuts, and some bananas for him," Schweitzer tells a native. "Perhaps that will quiet him down. He is quite dangerous still, our Jonas."

When the food comes, he sets it down, but Jonas shies away.

"We'll let him alone until he gets more used to us," says Schweitzer, coming out of the enclosure. "Later I want to wash out that nasty wound and see what's wrong with his leg." He looks up at the sky and quickly adds: "It will pour this afternoon, though. I'd better build him a shelter."

"May I take pictures when you do?" I ask.

"Certainly not," Schweitzer replies with firmness. "People would say, 'What an idiot that old fellow is always to pose for pictures.'"

"Dear Docteur," I answer. "I just thought that those who do not understand what your reverence for life philosophy means might get an idea by seeing you practicing it on Jonas, the wild pig."

But Dr. Schweitzer is adamant. No picture of him and the pig.

"May I come and watch you without a camera?" I ask.

"If you don't mind getting wet," he says. "I doubt I can finish before the rain starts. Come on! First we'll get some planks, then a piece of corrugated iron for the roof."

Schweitzer goes to work. A shelter for a sick, wounded pig must be built. For the moment, his health, the speech he is working on, all other considerations are irrelevant. The animal was brought to him by people who have learned and accepted the fact that among them is a white man who takes care of every man or beast, whatever the need.

While we are gathering the necessary materials, the rainstorm starts. Jonas, crouching in a corner, lunges at Schweitzer, and I am sick with fear. But Schweitzer nimbly places a plank in front of him, and talks quietly to the pig:

"You'd better get used to me, Jonas. I'm your friend."

Then he begins to shovel out a foundation for the planks.

"May I bring you a raincoat, Docteur?" I ask.

"No," he replies. "I can work better this way."

I stand there, my face pressed against the wire of the enclosure, in the pouring rain of the African jungle. I look down on the man busy with a shovel, busy with his hands creating a shelter, busy in his heart, in his great and peaceful heart, with the pain of a wounded animal. No tiredness shows in him. He stops only to wipe the rain from his eyes, never to straighten his back or to worry about getting drenched.

After two hours the shelter is finished. Then Dr. Percy joins him, and together they clean out and bandage the animal's wound, Schweitzer kneeling down to hold Jonas' head. After nibbling on some palm nuts, the pig is more calm and manageable. Four hours have passed, since Jonas was carried in, before Schweitzer leaves the enclosure.

Jonas, on a heap of leaves, rests comfortably under the roof of his new home.

12

Today I am up with the sun and take pictures of the boy ringing the morning bell, an hour before breakfast. He strikes it so many times that I lose count, but as soon as the chimes are over, life at the hospital begins to stir. The goats are let out of their night enclosure, and frolic and buck in the sunlight. Dr. Schweitzer appears on his porch, hangs up a small mirror on a hook, and shaves himself with a straight razor—he does not even use soap and water. I go over and ask him whether I can film him during this procedure, remarking that otherwise no one might believe that he shaves in this way.

"None need know," he replies, laughing. "You don't seriously think it could interest anyone, how I shave myself? Actually I learned this secret from the Turks, who are wise in such matters. Believe me, to shave dry is much better for the skin in this moist air than to soften it with soap and water."

When Schweitzer goes inside, I try to take pictures of the playful goats; but as soon as I'm set up to shoot, they sit down on their haunches and refuse to budge. Just then Schweitzer reappears on his way to breakfast. Instantly, all the goats get up.

"Very good," he says with a chuckle. "When the master of the house approaches, everybody should rise. That shows respect."

Schweitzer laughs, and I follow him into the dining room—where, incidentally, no one rises for anyone, since he would strongly object. Everybody is in good spirits and talks incessantly, especially the parrot, Habakkuk. Every so often Schweitzer tells it in French to shut up: *"Tais-toi! Tais-toi!"* In the middle of the meal, Madungo, the serving boy, suddenly puts his tray down. "I hear a hen giving," he explains, and rushes out the door to find the eggs. Schweitzer bursts out laughing and tells me it was the parrot imitating the noise of a hen laying an egg. Sure enough, a few moments later, Madungo, a sheepish smile on his face, comes back with empty hands. "That wretched bird! It fooled me again," he tells Schweitzer. "There are no eggs!"

"Parrots are very contrary," says Schweitzer. "I know a family who tried for months to teach their parrot just to say, *'Bon jour.'* They would repeat the phrase over and over again, but he would not say it. Then they got angry at the bird and told him how stupid he was: *'Comme vous êtes bête, imbécile!'* But the parrot stayed silent. One day a high church dignitary came for dinner. When he saw the parrot, he went over to the cage, stroked its neck, and said, 'What a beautiful bird you are.' The parrot took one look at the fellow and replied, *'Comme vous êtes bête, imbécile!'* "

Schweitzer's conversation romps from one subject to the next, sometimes playful, sometimes serious, but always alive with colorful detail. When we touch on the subject of churches, I happen to mention that the cathedral in Strasbourg is my favorite.

"Probably you didn't know that the Strasbourg Cathedral grew out of a mistake," he says.

"I did not," I concede.

"The church was originally designed to support two towers," he explains. "But later on one realized that the foundation was not strong enough, so the second tower had to be abandoned. But somehow this mistake makes it all the more beautiful. It is one of my favorites, too, that cathedral. Do you remember the expression of those figures around the entrance door? There is something very touching about them, especially about the Maria statue. These sculptures were all done by anonymous artists of the time. They were different from the artists of today. They were not so interested in making a name for themselves. They were mainly concerned that their work should be good, that it should express what they believed in. Do you know that Emperor Wilhelm was personally responsible for saving the cathedral?"

"No," I reply. "I'm afraid I did not learn much in school. And what I did learn I've forgotten."

"The cathedral was in actual danger of collapsing," continues Schweitzer. "The basic piles, which are made of wood, had dried out. When Emperor Wilhelm was informed of this, he realized that something must be done immediately. So he called together all the good men of his day, and he told them, 'If you cannot save the cathedral, I will have all of you hanged. But if you can save it, do not worry about the expense. I shall pay you what you wish.' Can you imagine such a thing happening today? Committees and subcommittees would discuss the whole issue until the cathedral had crumbled. The main thing, you see, is not to let wood dry out. If the wood is always kept wet, it's a very strong building material. They found that out when they built Venice. But that is another story. At heart, I've the soul of a schoolmaster. It's true, I do like to pass on information."

It is Saturday—cleaning day at the hospital—and after breakfast I watch all the beds being scrubbed and aired, and the bed pans, stretchers, and mats being spread out in the sun. Soap is used plentifully, and some of the patients' relatives, who live at the hospital, lend a hand in the energetic cleaning. But the one who enjoys the activities best is Horatius, a large baby gorilla that belongs to Dr. Percy. Horatius cavorts about, trying to mimic the motions of the workers. When one of the women cannot get rid of him, she dumps a bucket of cold water over him. He loves this, and after shaking himself dry, immediately comes back for more. Finally, Dr. Percy's wife comes to fetch the naughty fellow. Gently, she takes him by the hand and wanders off with him, like a mother leading her son. The Percys are very proud of their gorilla baby, Horatius.

After lunch I am off to the leper village, taking films of the cleaning and bandaging of the lepers' wounds, when a little boy appears, bearing a note. This is the Lambaréné telephone system. One reads the note, writes an answer, and the little boy runner carries it back to the sender. The note is from Mlle. Emma and reads:

"Come to the Doctor's house, but without your cameras. A loudspeaker will let us listen to the Doctor's speech while they record it over the Brazzaville radio."

I've forgotten all about the Doctor's speech. I so wish that I could take my cameras with me, but obedience is the first rule, and, back at the hospital, I sit under a mango tree, with Mlle. Emma and other staff members, to watch the technician setting up his equipment on the Doctor's porch. Soon the Doctor's voice comes through to us, and I hear him telling of the first trip he made to Lambaréné with his wife. On the other side of the yard the patients and hospital workers gather to hear the voice of their Grand Docteur. I don't think they catch much of what he is saying, but they listen in attentive silence, and when a familiar name is mentioned, a sudden murmur goes through the crowd, like approval. When the speech is over, the natives begin to sing. It's a song they do when someone they love parts from the hospital, or when he returns.

By dinnertime the Brazzaville technicians have left. I sit opposite Schweitzer, who buries his face in his hands, his eyes closed. He hardly eats, and when the nurse sitting at his right, Mlle. Kottman, pushes the food dishes toward him, he murmurs, "I am just too tired." The broadcast must have taken a lot out of him.

Mlle. Kottman invites me to visit her after dinner. She has shared in Dr. Schweitzer's work since 1927, and now devotes her time almost entirely to helping him with his correspondence. She is buried in mail. With a hopeless gesture she points to the stacks of unanswered letters and sighs:

"Long after I'm dead I feel I'll still be answering letters."

Three little cats play on her table, under the glow of a lamp. It is cozy in her room. When I tell her this, she replies:

"Yes. I love my room. But more and more, it becomes an office. It is very different now from the time I first came to help the Docteur. The world did not think of him much then, and I sometimes wonder if he was not better off. He was able to concentrate on his work. There is too much diversion now, and the hours he can spend on his books are all too few."

I know now what she means. I felt the same way myself when two Dutch journalists came the other day. I felt as though *they* were intruders, usurping the Doctor's time.

I'm about to go, but Mlle. Kottman brings out a picture book of her home in Alsace and urges me to look at it.

"You will like it if you go there," she says. "I won't be able to accompany the Docteur this year. There is too much work here. How I long sometimes to be back! It's been over two years now."

"I hope we shall be in the Alsace together someday," I tell her. "I would like you to think of me as a friend, and not just as another intruder."

"I know," she answers softly. "You and your companion have endeared yourselves to us. The Docteur is working on his mail now, too. But he will not mind if you stop by and wish him goodnight."

"No, no. Really not," I say.

"Ah, go on," she says. She presses me through the piano room, where the antelope cage is, on into Dr. Schweitzer's study.

"Mme. Anderson was afraid to say good-night to you," she tells him. "So I have brought her."

Schweitzer seems completely recovered from his exhaustion at the dinner table. He, too, is buried deep in mail, but his eyes are alert with humor.

"I am having a fine time with my mail tonight," he declares. "You've no idea of the requests I get. Here now is a gentleman in America who wants a gorilla, and inquires if I could sell him one. He would also like some wire netting for caging the gorilla, and says I am supposed to have the best wire netting in the world. Now where on earth could he have heard that? The strange part of it is that it's true. I know a nice old man in Strasbourg who makes the wire nettings for me in any design and strength I wish. Well, unless we send him Horatius, I'll have to decline the request for the gorilla. As for my Strasbourg wire netter, well, nothing in my life is a secret any more."

He is already picking up another letter.

"Here's one from a little girl in Germany," he says. "This is what she writes me: 'You are in Africa and I would like to come and visit you and play with the children at your hospital, but I know that when I grow up you will be dead.'"

Schweitzer laughs.

"She has sentiment, that child, hasn't she?" he says. "But she is a realist. She shall have an answer."

We leave Schweitzer to his correspondence—most of which is far less diverting than the letters he showed us—and I comment to Mlle. Kottman on Schweitzer's complete rejuvenation since dinner. She replies that the secret of his vitality is the frequency with which he shifts from one activity to another. When he's tired of writing, he goes out and works in the hot sun, building. When his feet are dragging from outdoor labor, he changes into his organ shoes and practices at the piano. When fatigue strikes him there, he returns to some desk work. Employing this rotating schedule, he's continually refreshed, instead of tired, by each new activity.

13

ON SUNDAY MORNINGS, regardless of weather, the church service is held outdoors, under the roofs of the wards in the main hospital street. The natives sit around in large groups. Many of the young mothers nurse their babies; goats, dogs, and cats wander among them or nurse their young. It is quite an informal affair—only a handful of the listeners hold Bibles in their hands.

Anyone of the staff who feels qualified can ask permission to hold the Sunday service. Today it is Mlle. Emma. She begins in French. Each sentence is translated first into the Fang dialect by a native standing on her left, then by another on her right who repeats it in Galois. The unconventional service is dignified and touching. This natural worship in the open street seems to embrace all of life. When Mlle. Emma's sermon is over, a hymn is sung by the congregation. Then the groups slowly disperse, and the patients return to their wards.

I walk a little way with Mlle. Emma. We have become very close during my stay. She seems to have a great deal of Dr. Schweitzer's spirit, a rare combination of kindness and strength. She has happy blue eyes, a tiny turned-up nose, and the liveliest, warmest expression. She tells me how she first heard of Dr. Schweitzer and how she had wanted to work with him in Africa ever since she was eight years old.

"I remember it so well," she says with a smile. "In school one day I heard a lecture about Dr. Schweitzer's mission station in Africa. It moved me so much that I rushed home to my parents and told them, 'That is what I want to do when I grow up.' My father frowned severely and told me to get such silly ideas out of my head. But my mother took me in her arms and said quietly, 'You will get there someday, if you wish hard enough.'"

Years later Mlle. Emma became a teacher in Alsace, and there she met a niece of Dr. Schweitzer's named Suzanne.

"One day I visited Suzanne, and I remarked how much I liked the white walls of her room. 'That's because my Uncle Albert loves white best of all colors.' Then she showed me a photograph of Dr. Schweitzer, and I decided to approach him with the idea of my helping him in Africa. I was twenty-five years old when I went to a talk he gave in Strasbourg, and approached him after the lecture. 'Are you a trained nurse?' he asked. 'No,' I told him. 'But any work you put me to, I will do with all my heart.'"

Schweitzer engaged her on the spot, and ever since she's been a kind of jack-of-all-trades in Lambaréné, including guardian angel to all newcomers.

"When Emma is in Lambaréné," Schweitzer always says, "I never have to worry. She does a better job than I."

Mlle. Emma invites me to accompany her to the babies' ward; some of the infants are orphans whose mothers have died during childbirth. When this happens, the rest of the family is often reluctant to bring up the baby, especially if it's a boy. Girls, since they can eventually be sold into marriage, are considered valuable property. But baby boys represent nothing but an additional expense. Some of the hospital orphans are twins, who are considered especially bad luck by the natives. This superstition is so deep-rooted that when twins are born one of them is sometimes murdered by the family. Dr. Schweitzer has made it known that he will undertake the responsibility of bringing up twins and even give a special present to their family. In this way he has been able gradually to eliminate the taboo.

Then we visit one of the nurses, Irmgard, who is so attached to the babies that she keeps eight cribs of them in her room. Irmgard says that there are some nights when there's hardly a moment that she isn't awakened by one of her charges crying. But she cannot bring herself to part with them. To make matters worse, she insists that any sick baby be immediately taken to her room, where it stays until fully recovered. Since her room is next to those of the other hospital personnel, especially Dr. Schweitzer's, I ask if she doesn't receive occasional complaints.

"Oh, there's plenty of grumbling," she replies. "But it's always good natured, and since Dr. Schweitzer never complained, no one else dares to—openly, at least."

On our way back we visit the wards where white patients are

taken care of and chat with an elderly lady who's been recovering from a severe nervous breakdown.

"I've spent years in the interior of Africa with my husband," she tells us. "Life in the jungle is so hard that it finally got me. I came to the hospital a physical and mental wreck. I was so nervous that I began to cry any time the slightest problem presented itself. I could not arrive at the tiniest decision. I was making the life of my husband, as well as mine, a hell. My body was riddled by malaria, dysentery, ulcers, and anemia. I was put to bed here a bundle of unhappiness. Each day Dr. Schweitzer came to see me. Several times each day. He never let a day go by without coming in to say 'Good-night.' Due to his care, I'm able to walk, talk, and think again. The only way I can repay him is to get well and try to live in his spirit, to forget my ego and look for opportunities to help others who are badly off."

Sunday is a day I especially enjoy in Lambaréné because of the additional chance provided to talk with Schweitzer at teatime. In fact, besides mealtimes, Sunday afternoon tea is the closest thing to an actual social hour in the whole routine of the hospital, and doctors and nurses who are off duty drop into the dining room to meet guests or relax with one another. Some of the nurses read old numbers of magazines. Others are studying French. One group sits together rehearsing a song to be done in harmony for the Doctor's birthday. I follow Mlle. Emma as she proceeds from group to group, inquiring how everyone is getting on. We search out Schweitzer, who is discussing with a Dutch journalist the problem of ventilating buildings in Africa.

"What one needs is air," he is saying. "If one is shut up in a room without ventilation, it is very demoralizing."

A Swiss nurse, Mlle. Koch, says:

"Docteur, tell about your charge on the boat that time, which illustrates the point."

"Ah yes," says Schweitzer. "I once had to transport a mentally ill man by boat to Europe—"

"That was a trip on which you were supposed to rest and work on your book and be otherwise undisturbed," says Mlle. Koch.

"That's beside the point," says Schweitzer. "In any case, the room they'd appropriated for the poor fellow was below deck in the bow of the ship. It was so murderously hot, especially during the day, that I simply could not leave him there. I kept him on deck with me and had to watch him carefully all the time. Then I asked the captain of the boat to come with me to his room. I took him inside and closed the door behind us. The captain almost suffocated. Yet even after that he did not assign the sick man another room. So one night I took my patient down there and I told him: 'I am not going to give you any sedative. When the heat becomes unbearable, you go right ahead and tear apart everything which is not bolted down, the whole padding and all. This is obviously the only way we can effect a change and show them that you need different quarters.' The next day the room, which was like a jail cell, was in such a state that the captain arranged for another room. I had no more trouble with my sick friend. With a little reason and much heart, one can change many things, or move mountains."

I remark on the warm family feeling of Sunday teatime in Lambaréné, and Schweitzer says it was like that in Günsbach when he was growing up.

"Yes, we always had friends in the house when I was a boy," he recalls. "I had three sisters and a brother, and we were always allowed to bring home as many friends as we wished. Father and Mother never minded the house being full of guests. In fact, I have never lived alone. I like being surrounded by people. There is none of the hermit instinct in me. I don't understand people who build a house way off from their neighbors. A friendly neighbor within reach is a good thing."

After Schweitzer leaves, we talk to Dr. Percy and his wife.

"We have to be home soon," he tells us, smiling. "Horatius, my demanding gorilla, is expecting us. He is just like a child, and we are like proud and fussy parents when it comes to him. Sometime would you take some pictures of him for us?"

"If you wish, I'll do it right now," I tell him.

On the way to the Percys' house I mention how much I envy those who can stay and work in Lambaréné.

"The Lambaréné bug has bitten you," says Dr. Percy. "I can see that. It's the same way with most of us. But you should realize that working here, day in and day out, does present problems. One of them is the lack of privacy. This may strike you as strange. To be way off in the jungle and miss your privacy. But it is a fact. The jungle around us forces us together like people on an ocean island."

When we reach their house, Horatius is jubilant and makes a beeline for Dr. Percy's arms, then wraps both paws around his face. But he doesn't stay put for long. He's a good subject, as funny and natural as they come.

"I wish Dr. Schweitzer were as relaxed as Horatius in front of a camera," I tell the Percys. "My trouble is that Schweitzer is really very camera shy, always stiffening up and posing. I wonder if I'll ever get him on film as he really is."

When I get back to *Sans Souci,* the door won't open. I fumble about with the key, but it just won't turn. Then I realize that I've taken away the key to *Hinterindien* by mistake! I rush out there, and find an enormous line of people waiting. What indignant looks I get when it's learned I am the culprit!

At dinner Dr. and Mrs. Nägeli invite me to visit them later in the evening. On my way to their room I pass Dr. Schweitzer in the dark.

"*Qui est là?*" he asks.

"It's me, Erica," I reply.

"I just wondered if you'd like to be with me when I rehearse," he says. "You had no pictures of me today, and I thought it might please you."

"I would love to," I reply. "But I've promised to visit the Nägelis."

"Well, run down and tell them you'll be half an hour late," he says.

I immediately do this and come back. Until then I had always visited in the room which contains his bed, washstand, desk, and bookshelves. Now I hear him already playing on the piano. I walk through a tiny connecting corridor into the next room. This one is even smaller than the study-bedroom. Opposite the door stands the piano with its pedal attachments for bass notes; on top of it is a kerosene lamp with a green shade, softening the light on Schweitzer's face. In back of him the whole wall is lined with shelves tightly packed with books. On the right, toward the river, is an enclosure with three small antelopes in it. A bundle of sweet-smelling fresh leaves is spread out on the floor, and the antelopes munch happily on them, while Schweitzer plays. On the left of

75 ६৯

the piano is a smaller cage for the two chimps, Romeo and Juliet. During the day they always walk arm in arm, and now they are sleeping in each other's arms. Another cage on a shelf, which contains Habakkuk, the parrot, is covered with a cloth. I slip behind Schweitzer and try to settle silently on a low chest. But he stops playing.

"Sit next to me," he says. "There is plenty of room on the piano bench—no discussion—that's an order."

He takes my hand and sits me down. But I do it so clumsily that my feet hit the base pedals, which give out a muffled croak. I jump up.

"Easy. Legs down," he says, and begins to play.

In front of him is the music sheet, and he holds a small yellow pencil between his lips. Ever so often he stops to write in some numbers over the notes. He plays a chord over and over, writing numbers, erasing them, then trying it again. When he is satisfied, he nods, "That's it." I sit quiet as a mouse, holding my breath.

"I write all the possible finger combinations," he explains. "Listen to this. If I play with the fourth finger, it's easier than when I use the third. Can you hear the difference?"

"I'm not sure I can," I stammer. "It all sounds wonderful to me."

Fortunately, he does not hear my reply; he is concentrating again on the music, like a young student, eagerly and earnestly rehearsing. After half an hour he stops and says:

"Now I will play something by heart."

He puts away the score, takes the pencil out of his mouth, and closes his eyes. A few seconds later he starts a piece by César Franck.

"This is something wonderful but difficult," he says quietly. "One has to wring it out of oneself."

His feet and hands play in unison, his whole body vigorously participating; but his face is utterly calm, as though it were to him the most peaceful relaxation.

When the last chord fades away, he puts his hand on mine and says:

"So. Now go visiting."

With this he moves over to get up. But I cannot leave without letting him know what this has meant to me. I look up at him and helplessly grope for words.

"It's all right, Erica," he says. "You don't need to say anything, for I know what you want to say. Let me tell you something. Someday, I will have you sit next to me when I play on one of the great organs in Europe. In a cathedral, at night, perhaps Strasbourg. And when the sound fills the church, then you will be truly pleased with your new friend."

He walks over to the indoor antelope pen, kneels down, and takes some bread out of his pocket. He pats one of them.

"This is Bichette," he says. "She is my favorite. Actually, she is getting a little too fat. She is getting a *bon point,* but she has a soul. The other two always remain so slim some film stars might envy them. Good-night, Bichette. Good-night, Jagaguno, and good-night—well, this one has no name yet, and perhaps I will call her Erica. Would you like that? I am a bit worried about her —when she was brought to me her foot was badly infected. It was caught in a trap in which her mother was killed. A native brought her here. I hope we can save her leg."

"I think it would be very fitting if this one is called Erica," I reply joyfully. "Because she will be especially grateful, and that is what I am. Good-night, dear Dr. Schweitzer."

When I leave his room, he follows and calls after me:

"Have you got your light, so that you don't step on any snakes?"

"Yes, thank you," I reply. "I have my light with me."

I slowly walk down to the Nägelis' house, though I'd prefer to be back in my room, by myself, with my memories of this evening filled with peace.

14

EARLY TODAY everybody meets at the white patients' ward to sing to one of the little boys born at the hospital. It is his fifth birthday, each one spent and celebrated at the hospital.

Armed with all my equipment, I get set up at a strategic point from which I can see Dr. Schweitzer and the staff members. The group stands outside the small room where the boy and his parents have spent the night, and they begin to sing a German hymn. When the hymn is over, Dr. Schweitzer enters the room and congratulates the mother of the child. The little boy presses himself against Schweitzer's knees, and when he picks him up, begins to play with his mustache. Then the others enter. Each one offers friendly words. Then Schweitzer and Mlle. Emma lead the boy by the hand into the dining room.

The big table is set as usual, but opposite Dr. Schweitzer is a high chair for the child, and around his cup and plate are presents from the staff and the natives. Nothing is bought. Everything is handmade: simple carvings, an ebony elephant and an antelope made of ivory, a portrait of Lisi the goose painted on a mat. Madungo brings two fried eggs, and the child digs into them with glee.

Schweitzer brings a photograph of the hospital with him and signs it in his characteristically neat handwriting: "To Michel whom we welcomed at the Lambaréné hospital when he was born. With my best thoughts." The mother takes it for the boy. She looks proud and grateful.

"We will treasure it always, dear Grand Docteur," she says in a low voice.

Mr. Hug has decorated the dining room with his paintings, and Schweitzer wanders from one to the other, admiring them.

"He has become the Lambaréné court painter," he says to me. "How would you like to be the court photographer?"

"Court photographer? That would suit me fine," I reply, scratching at my leg without noticing it.

"What are you doing?" Schweitzer asks. "Do you think that is how royal photographers behave? Your court etiquette lacks a great deal."

It's true. I'm riddled with mosquito bites and find myself scratching everywhere. Everybody has some bites, but at least they do not complain about them, and they refrain from scratching. But after Schweitzer's remark, I realize that I scratch myself incessantly and must resemble a monkey.

Shyly, I ask Dr. Schweitzer whether I may take some motion pictures in the dining room. The days have been rolling on; we are leaving in less than a week, and I have little material of him as yet. But Schweitzer refuses.

"Not today," he says. "We have guests. Perhaps tomorrow."

Two French doctors have arrived. They sit opposite Schweitzer at lunch. It is very hot.

"This is the time of the equinox," Schweitzer remarks. "Day and night are equally long. The sun is exactly at its zenith. It means bad weather."

"For how long?" I ask.

"The next few days," he answers. "But don't let it spoil your appetite. Here it never rains for a full day. It's like a child's dream come true—rain at night, but sunshine all day."

I sip a glass of water mixed with fresh lime juice.

"It's hard to resist the good food of your table, even if I can't take pictures," I say. "I eat much more here than I do at home and certainly more than I deserve."

"The unsalted food of Lambaréné is much healthier for you," says Schweitzer. "I was startled when I visited America. I saw even little children grabbing the salt shaker and dumping it onto their food. That is not good. I learned a lot from some early studies of the salt-free diet. Not to eat salt helps the circulation. One does not retain so much water in one's system. One also is less thirsty. That is a big advantage here or anywhere in the tropics. I hardly drink any water, despite the heat, since I learned to do without salt."

It starts to pour now, and Mlle. Emma, who has been in Lambaréné to fetch the mail, comes to the table, drenched to the bone. Schweitzer talks to her in the Alsatian dialect.

"Did the mail get wet?" he asks teasingly. "And the natives who paddled? And you?"

With a twinkle in his eyes, he turns to us.

"You see," he says, "this is the way to ask. Always in the proper sequence of importance."

While coffee is being served, I do get permission to take a few stills with my Rolleiflex. But, as usual, Schweitzer straightens up, getting ready to pose. He runs his fingers through his unruly hair and puts on the formal face for being photographed. How will I ever break this down? After Dr. Schweitzer leaves the dining room, I stay on with Dr. Percy.

"That you are able to speak with the Docteur in his own language has played a big part in his giving you permission for the film," he says. "It's a very important thing; he feels most at home speaking German or the Alsatian dialect."

Julia and I run back to our room. It is pouring buckets by now. I want to lie down for a siesta but am so fascinated by the *"tornade,"* the storm, that I brave the rain and take films of it. In a few minutes I am drenched.

Letter writing and the cleaning of cameras occupies the afternoon. Later I wander down to the hospital and visit some of the natives who have become my friends. My pockets are bulging with candy, and they grin broadly when I approach. "Bonbon! Bonbon!" they call, and adults as well as children enjoy the sweets.

In the pharmacy I find Toni van Leer, a lovely young Dutch nurse. She weighs and measures white powders and bottles them neatly.

"Our medicine is cheaper if we bottle it ourselves," she says. "In a few minutes I'll be giving drugs to my charges. If you wish, you might film it."

A long line of patients is forming. One by one they pass Toni, their mouths wide open. Toni pours in the medicine and then gives them a bit of water to swallow.

"This is the only way we're sure it's inside them," she laughs. "If we left it to them, they would take a whole bottle at once, or throw it into the river, or sell it to someone else."

The downpour continues with tremendous force. Down by the

river I film a canoe fighting with the angry waves. People are running to their wards. A group of goats gallop for shelter; one small kid slows up its mother, heedless of the storm, trying to suckle. I end the sequence with a shot of huge palm leaves lashing against the tree trunks in an eerie dance.

Later, when the storm has passed and everything looks like the first day of creation, glistening and beautiful, the courtyard swarms with activities. Men have come with a big crocodile to sell its meat. It is hung up and weighed and then carefully cut up. Women carry bundles of bananas on their heads and sell them to the cook. The boys rush to and fro with their vegetables. The carpenter is sighing loudly while he cuts wood, and even the mute shoemaker makes eyes at the girls who work on the laundry bench. Schweitzer passes me, while I stand in the midst of all this, my camera rolling.

"How do you like the odor of that crocodile meat?" he asks. "You know what they say about it here: 'It's the meat we eat, not the smell!' "

He mingles with the rest of the busy crowd, and I admire the vigorous step, the youthful walk he still has.

Next morning at breakfast Mlle. Emma tells us that a small poisonous viper was found in the stable with Lisi the goose; though they must have slept side by side, Lisi was unharmed.

"We must never forget the danger of snakes," Schweitzer says. "It is most important when entering or leaving a room that they don't slither in with you. Keep the doors closed at all times. Just recently a young teacher stayed with us. Though we all told her to be careful, a snake was found curled under her pillow in the morning. The woman could have died. Those small green ones are very poisonous. We have many different kinds here. Some do not attack. Some live in trees. They are born there and wait for birds to come flying into the branches. The snakes cannot descend. They live up there like the early Christian hermits. Oh, I know a lovely story about a snake, but it ends in a sad way. Shall I tell it to you?"

There are shouts of approval, so Schweitzer begins:

"A European hunter deep in the interior came upon a wounded boa constrictor. Its skin had been torn off in parts, and it was mauled and bleeding, obviously from an attack by wild animals.

81 ॐ

'I will nurse you until you are well again,' the hunter said to the boa. 'But on one condition. You will get no live flesh to eat—only scraps from our table.'

"The hunter cleaned and bandaged its wounds. For two weeks the snake fasted. Then it began to nibble on the meat left over from meals. When the camp moved on, my friend, the leader of the expedition, picked two boys who were not much good for other tasks, and ordered them to pack the boa into a basket. With the basket swinging from a pole, the two boys carried the boa between them. But every time the caravan stopped at a resting place, the two boys arrived long after the others. At last they were so late that the hunter sent another boy to see what was holding them up. He spied the boa wriggling along nonchalantly while the two boys swung the empty basket between them. 'Aren't you supposed to be carrying the snake?' asked the runner. 'Well, he got to be pretty heavy,' they replied. 'While we were having a smoke, the boa came out of the basket and walked in the right direction, so now we just follow her.'

"A nice story so far," continues Schweitzer, "but here is the sad ending. One day my friend had a visitor who came for breakfast, proudly announcing that he had shot a boa constrictor, and thereby saved them all from being killed. It was the good old boa, who'd become so civilized that chickens and geese could run around her without fear. Isn't that sad? And the moral of the story—well, I'll let you figure that out by yourself."

I ask whether I can take some shots in the dining room yet. All look. Schweitzer answers:

"Yes. Today we have no strangers with us, so it's all right. Now the trick will be to move closely together so that we can all get into the picture."

I find it funny that he directs the scene. I say yes to everything because it obviously gives him pleasure to take over the arrangement.

"Where did you learn directing?" I ask him.

"That talent was given me by the three fairy godmothers who stood around my cradle," he says, smiling. "But two things I have never been able to learn. One is to say no, and the other is to write a short letter or a short introduction. I was once asked by friends to write an introduction for someone whose name was not known. To help it along a bit, I started to write the introduction but ended up with another complete book. It cost me two years!"

I ask the Doctor whether he has seen many films.

"In my whole life, six," he replies. "I understand nothing about this art form."

"Were they features or documentaries?" I inquire.

"Features, I suppose," he replies. "Because in all of them the hero and heroine got together in the end. I saw them on the boat coming from Europe, and I must say I am more impressed by the open sky, the stars, and the ocean. Also, on the screen, everything rolls too fast. It hurts my eyes."

"In my Grandma Moses film the tempo was kept much slower than usual," I tell him.

"Grandma Moses is quite a lady," Dr. Schweitzer says. "She paints nostalgia."

Mlle. Emma cuts in:

"When you are really old, Docteur, maybe you will take up painting too? Or directing movies?"

We all laugh, and Schweitzer resumes:

"You know what I would really like to do if I had time? Just once or twice, to get up without feeling tired and to go to bed without knowing how many things are still left undone. What a luxury that would be! You know that basically I am very lazy. That is why I must work so hard. But everybody thinks I am by nature industrious. If you knew how much worry my father had with me! I could not learn to read and write easily, and my father always said to me, 'Albert, if you would only make an effort to read and write so that you can at least become the mailman in Günsbach.'"

"What did your father then say when you became famous?" I ask.

"Well," replies Schweitzer. "He read my philosophical books and said, 'About the eschatological writings, you are probably right, but no one will believe you.' Later, when I studied so much, he complained, 'Albert always lives in extremes. First, he is so lazy no one can get him to study. Now he is so busy no one can get him to take a walk.'"

"Were you lazy with your music, too?" I ask.

"No. I always loved organ music and organs," he replies. "I

always burn with fury when organs are placed in a wrong spot in a church. Like families who hide ugly daughters behind the stove, some organs are hidden. But organs should be seen, and the music allowed to stream out. In Chartres, in Strasbourg, in Freiburg— there they are placed right."

When I ask him if he likes to make recordings, he explains:

"That is *really* hard work. If one hits one wrong note in the end, one has to start from the beginning again. And one can hear it only after the whole recording is finished. I happened to make most of my recordings in London. When I went there in 1930, I searched for three solid days to find the most beautiful-sounding organ. At last, in a small church, I found it. But the rector resisted at first and told me it would disturb him if I made recordings there. So I had to devise all kinds of arguments. I even told him that should the church ever be destroyed at least the sound of the organ would survive. Finally, he gave me permission to do my work there during the nights. I had to rehearse for three nights, and half the time I was on stepladders stuffing cotton wool into the windows so there'd be no vibrations. During the war, the church did burn down, but the records survived."

"You see, Docteur," I say, "I have the same argument with my film. It will remain and tell the world of your work."

"You are a sly one," he replies. "Whatever way the conversation turns, you always get back to your film. But if it pleases you, I shall leave you with that triumphant thought."

15

THE DAY BEFORE we leave is Easter Sunday—March 25, 1951. Before breakfast I sort out the clothes I want to leave as gifts for the patients and nurses. I give them to Mlle. Emma to distribute as she thinks best—dresses, slips, and stockings. I also insist on leaving two hundred dollars with her to help cover the cost of our stay.

"The Docteur will be very cross when I tell him," Mlle. Emma protests. But it seems little enough, considering how long we stayed and the size of our appetites!

Schweitzer arrives at the breakfast table a bit late today.

"Your last day in Lambaréné," he says quietly, nodding toward Julia and me. Then to Mlle. Emma, he says: "Come! Make them a bit gayer. Tell them the story of how you were once kissed by Emperor Wilhelm."

Emma laughs and begins:

"When I was eleven years old, the Emperor came passing through my village. There was great excitement at the railroad station. Everybody was crowding around his train. The Emperor already had one foot inside his compartment, when I squeezed through the crowds without asking permission. I had picked a bunch of flowers in the meadow—some lilies of the valley—and I placed them in his hand and recited a little poem. Then the Emperor patted my face—"

"And kissed her," Schweitzer interrupts. " 'It was the most beautiful day of my life,' " he teases, mimicking Emma's enthusiasm. Then as I laugh, he teases me, saying: " 'Almost as beautiful as the time I stayed in Lambaréné with the Grand Docteur!' "

I laugh, but the sad truth is that I feel just as he says.

"Your plane leaves tomorrow morning at nine-thirty," says Schweitzer, more seriously. "You should leave here at seven-thirty. A truck will take you to the airport from the place where the pirogue lands. But if the road is very wet you may have to walk the last few hundred yards."

I have the feeling that Schweitzer dwells on these physical details of the departure to make the event itself less upsetting to us.

"I can't even remember where we arrived," I tell him. "I was so nervous at meeting you that I noticed little except how fast my heart was beating."

"Yes, yes." Schweitzer smiles. "You did not know then how quickly you would wrap the old grouchy bear around your little finger and fulfill your wish to film here."

I spend much of the afternoon composing a message for the guest book. Julia tells me it is much too flowery and emotional.

At dinnertime each of us is given an Easter egg, quite a luxury. To get an egg one usually has to be sick or have a birthday. After the hymn Schweitzer says:

"Once again an Easter Sunday has passed." Then he looks out of the window into the night and I sense his consciousness of time. His eyes seem to ask: "How much is left? How many more years?" He reads a sentence from a letter of St. Paul: *"Though our physical body decays, our inner soul renews itself from day to day."*

When he leaves the table, he takes his old hat from its hook, and coming by me, asks:

"You care to be with me for a little, yes?"

"When may I come?" I ask.

"Right now. Bring your light with you."

Crossing the yard, we look up at the stars.

"In nature most people search for the unusual, the unexpected," he tells me. "But it's the monotony of nature that's most dear to me. Like the monotony of my daily routine. I look forward to knowing what will happen on Monday and that the same thing will happen on Tuesday and again on Wednesday. I am not much of a traveler. To pack up and live out of a suitcase is something I do only when I have to."

In his study he hangs up his hat, lights a kerosene lamp, and washes his hands.

"Let's go into the piano room," he says.

There we talk a bit of the film. I tell him that when the film is finished, I shall consider the material and the decision what to do with it solely his.

"No," Schweitzer replies. "This I do not ask and will not accept. The material is yours. Just wait until my death. After that you may do with it what you wish. Yes. You will hear of my death either by telegram or in the newspapers. Then do whatever you feel is right, but before you start crying, check with me—one can't always trust newspaper reports.

"Please," I say. "Don't speak of your death. I hope and pray that there may be many years before that."

"But at my age death can come fast," Schweitzer continues. "I see the possibility with calm. In any case, I shall write to Jerome Hill and explain this to him, too."

"You don't have to explain anything to Jerome—"

"Stop that!" he interrupts. "You cannot tell me what I have or have not to do. That is clear. But one thing I want to say to you now." He looks me full in the face, and gently continues: "It is a strange thing that when I was shown the letter to you refusing your request to film, something went through my head—I'm not sure what—but I had to add 'Come.'"

"This word from you is the only reason for my being here," I tell him. "I clung to it like a drowning swimmer."

"I am glad you have liked it here."

Then he gives me a present: a large white apron with the words HÔPITAL SCHWEITZER written on it.

"Let's try it on," he says, putting it over my head. "Yes. I'm afraid it's a bit big on you. You'll have to pin it up. But traveling around alone in the world, it will be a good thing for you to have, at least while you are in Africa."

In the morning we leave right after breakfast. I manage to keep my tears from showing until the boat draws away from the river-bank. The paddlers seem accustomed to visitors crying when they leave, and they chant softly as the boat turns round the bend.

16

W HEN I GOT BACK to New York in mid-May, the developed films were a terrible disappointment—much
of the emulsion had melted away in the humid climate. What
had looked lush and green in Lambaréné was gray and un-
exciting on film. The soft, dark shades of the African jungle had
not come through. I burst into tears.

But in the next week, as more material came back from the
laboratory, the outlook became a little brighter. And I'd had
better luck with the still photos—so much so that I began to
prepare an album for Dr. Schweitzer. I was greatly encouraged
at the same time by a letter I received from the Doctor himself.
He wrote:

Dear Erica:

It is past midnight. The whole day I had to write letters but I want
this to go off, I hope, with the plane that leaves tomorrow morning. I
think with pleasure of you and your companion. The two last days
you should have been here! Building was in progress. Workmen carried stones and cement in cases. We only had a very short pause for
lunch and work went on into the night. This will keep on for several
days. So it was years ago, day by day, when I built the hospital. But
this time it will last only ten days—repair work and the like! Don't
forget Lambaréné and its stillness, and come again. Get a savings box,
and into it put all the money you would otherwise spend uselessly on
candy or cigarettes until there's enough for a third-class ticket on a
petrol steamer. There's one that goes directly from America to Douala.
And take good care of the hospital apron.

Best regards,
Albert Schweitzer

When my photo album was finished, I bound it in green
leather, inscribed it to Dr. Schweitzer, and sent it off to him in
Günsbach where he was visiting. I hoped to join him there and
do some more shooting, but this depended entirely on the response. Eagerly, I waited for a letter. The end of June, it came:

To the Court Photographer of Lambaréné:

We are in an ecstasy of joy! Especially Dr. Schweitzer. Your album arrived in good shape. What an abundance of beauty. Impossible to find words. The last pictures of the album, head and hands of Dr. Schweitzer, how moving!

On the 28th of July, the anniversary of Bach's death, Dr. Schweitzer will play a concert in St. Thomas' Church in Strasbourg. You should be present! It would also be good if you could be here in Günsbach between the 7th and 14th of August, because there will be much music in our house. I would like to arrange for a room for you in Münster, a few minutes away from Günsbach—let me know if this is feasible. During the summer it is quite difficult to get rooms, unless I make reservations at once.

We will be in Strasbourg from the 23rd of July to the 2nd of August. If you send me a wire I will order rooms at once. Forgive my matter-of-fact writing, dear Court Photographer, best regards, and thanks to Mr. Hill. Everything was a wonderful stroke of fate.

Yours,
Emma Martin

I was overjoyed. So was Jerome Hill who decided to come with me. How different this would be from my first trip to Africa! Now I was expected—almost, it seemed, wanted! We accepted the invitation and planned to arrive in Strasbourg July 26.

"It will be better not to meet Schweitzer before the concert," I say to Jerome when we get to Strasbourg. "He must be pressed for time, and I don't want to disturb him."

Jerome and I stroll around Strasbourg, visiting the cathedral, the university, and the Thomas Gstaaden where Schweitzer had lived; but around the rue de Grenier where he now resides we make a big detour. For some reason, I do not want to risk running into the Doctor by chance.

The night of the concert we arrive at St. Thomas Church at six o'clock. Hundreds of people are already gathered there, standing outside the church, though the concert does not start until seven-thirty. We've inched our way forward to about the fourth row of standees, when Schweitzer arrives. His European clothes strike me as very strange: a black Loden coat, a large black hat, an old-fashioned collar and black tie. He looks very much the proverbial German professor, quite different from the worker of

Lambaréné with his sun helmet, sand-colored trousers, and the white, open-collared shirt.

He walks briskly, waves at the crowd, but does not stop to talk with anyone before entering the church. A few minutes later the church door opens and Mme. Martin beckons to someone in the crowd. I turn instinctively to look for that someone behind, not believing she could mean me. But I feel myself pushed forward.

"Yes, I mean you," Mme. Martin says. "The Docteur told me that he made you a promise. Follow me."

Schweitzer is already in the organ loft when we reached him.

"An elephant does not forget," he says, taking my hand. "Didn't I promise you that someday you would be with me when I played on a beautiful church organ, instead of an out-of-tune piano with pedal attachments?"

The concert seems to me the most beautiful I have ever heard. When it is over, it appears that the entire population of Strasbourg has come for a glimpse of their Docteur. Police squads are on hand to protect him from the applauding crowds engulfing him, but Schweitzer calls out to the police:

"No, no, this would be the end if I needed protection from my friends in Strasbourg. Please leave us alone."

For many hours he writes autograph after autograph. Later, still pursued by hundreds of the townsfolk, he goes to a little restaurant, the Marne, where he plans to dine quietly with friends and relatives. Jerome Hill and I are to meet him there.

"So you are the generous soul who let this creature come to Lambaréné despite all my objections" are the words with which Schweitzer takes Jerome's hand. "The girl's stubborn as a dog," he continues. "Like a flea which digs in where the dog can't scratch. That's the way she is. I just could not refuse her."

Jerome, whose German is as good as his French, proceeds to outline our plans. Although Schweitzer does not want to go into details about the completion and use of the film, he invites us to Günsbach for the following weeks, where he is to play his organ which has been rebuilt under his supervision. There is one point on which the three of us are in absolute agreement: the film must not be rushed. Authenticity, not time, is our main concern.

The drive from Strasbourg to Günsbach, passing through Colmar and into the Münster Valley, makes an enchanting trip. Lovely, quaint little villages, each with its own church and tall steeple, are nestled into the Vosges Mountains. Kaysersberg, Schweitzer's birthplace, has not changed much since the nineteenth century. The houses, one or two stories high, have retained their charm. On the upper left of a street leading into the woods is the house where he was born and the church where his father was a Protestant minister.

When we arrive in Günsbach Dr. Schweitzer introduces me to his wife. Mrs. Helene Schweitzer welcomes me warmly and in spite of her frailty and ill health invites me on many occasions during my visit to spend a little time with her alone. She likes to sit in an old-fashioned easy chair by the window in the downstairs living room, looking out over the garden and meadow behind the house. I love to listen as she speaks of the early days in Lambaréné, when she, in full health then, helped her husband to lay the cornerstones of their hospital. Her beautiful sad eyes shine when she invokes the memories of those first years in Africa, and one can sense her longing to return.

Rhena, Schweitzer's only daughter, comes frequently from nearby Switzerland with her husband and their four children. Many times we all go into the vineyards surrounding Günsbach to pick the delicious ripe grapes, or set out for picnics in the Vosges Mountains. I intensely enjoy the charm of Alsace and its people as I come to know Schweitzer's immediate family.

While in Günsbach, Jerome and I are struck by the number of people who keep streaming into the Schweitzer house. They come from everywhere—neighbors and friends from the valley, from the nearby cities—Colmar, Strasbourg, Mulhouse, and Paris. But there are almost as many from other countries, too, from Denmark, the Netherlands, Belgium, Sweden, India, England, America . . . a constant flow. And Schweitzer is always ready to receive anyone who has a question to pose, a problem to discuss, whatever it might be. He remarks that the reason he became a minister instead of striving for a professorial career was simply to have more personal and daily contact with people than the academic life would permit. Even now, while he is home, he is asked to aid all kinds of human suffering. A father comes to him, in deep despair about placing his Mongoloid child in a mental home; a young bride terribly disillusioned by her marriage; a lonely widow. Schweitzer offers far more than general advice. There is something deeply and distinctly personal in his dealings with people. When the widow is leaving him, for instance, Schweitzer follows her a few steps away from the house. "This is the spot where your husband said good-by to me for the last time," Schweitzer tells her gently. For some astonishing, inexplicable reason, he remembers the day, the month, and the year of the event, though it happened thirteen years ago!

Downstairs in his bed-workroom, Schweitzer does his writing, while on the second floor in the office, basketfuls of correspondence accumulate, which he tries to catch up on in the evenings. He takes walks every day, usually with some of his visitors, up to the Kanzenrain, where he used to do his schoolwork as a boy. And every day he goes to church to play the organ, his beloved instrument. Informal performances are often held in his home. Music students get solid criticism as well as encouragement from Schweitzer. Even accomplished artists do not escape this, if he feels it will help.

Schweitzer's natural kindness and charm make Jerome and me feel as if we have been his friends for many years. When Jerome and I first hear Schweitzer play on the Günsbach organ, we both decide to film and record a Schweitzer concert right there, rather than in a large cathedral. This is the organ that Schweitzer loves, and since he has agreed that a scene of his playing should be included in the film, we immediately make the necessary arrangements. Jerome cables a sound engineer in New York to bring a big recording truck to Günsbach. The date set for recording is October 6. Because of customs formalities, Jerome has to go to Paris, but I am left in Günsbach, with my camera, to roam, be around Schweitzer, and take as many pictures as I can.

Because I have a car and do not want to be just a useless "guest," I offer to do the food shopping for the house, and thus lift at least one responsibility off the busy shoulders of the lady who cooks for the Günsbach family. Mme. Martin has her hands full, too, never quite knowing how many guests to expect for a meal. More often than not, Schweitzer, just a few minutes before lunch or dinner, will call upstairs: "Add a little water to the soup. Three more coming!"

Our huge recording truck arrives in the main street of Güns-bach on October 6. At first the population do not know what is going on. They come out of their houses in curious bewilderment, and by the time we've decided that the best place for the truck is by the village dumpheap, just below the church, we are surrounded by onlookers. The village children are especially fascinated by the placement of the cables in and around the church. Even Schweitzer shakes his head in amazement when he sees the elaborate installations. His earlier recordings were made on wax plates which cannot be played back until after they are processed and pressed. With our tapes, however, we can record Schweitzer's playing and run it back for him moments later. The first time we do this, Schweitzer's face registers surprise, then interest, then obvious enthusiasm. It means, too, that he can immediately play over passages that he is not pleased with.

A day or so later Schweitzer invites Jerome and me for a walk. "I have been thinking," he says. "I am so delighted with your equipment that I would like to record a whole program of Bach, Widor, César Franck, and Mendelssohn. I have always wanted to do this in my little church, here on my organ. Would you be willing to co-operate?"

Naturally, we are very pleased. Schweitzer wants to do the bulk of the recordings the following fall. He wants to rehearse the pieces by heart and not be hampered by having to read the scores. It will be a tremendous undertaking for him, in addition to all his hospital work, but the project seems to please him immensely. And for me it means assurance that I can be back again the next summer!

For a week he rehearses every morning. In the afternoon we film and record. When the weather is especially beautiful, we drive to the mountains to take pictures of the landscape, the people working in the fields, and the women washing their laundry in the stream that runs through the village. We soon make friends with most of the village people, and the children surround the truck and dance to the music of Bach. Our plan is to devote a whole sequence of film to showing the reaction of Schweitzer's neighbors to his organ playing. (Eventually this had to be cut out. We just could not spare the footage—there was so much else to show in a film of only an hour and a half duration.)

In the middle of October the truck leaves with Jerome, Julia, the sound engineer and his wife, all perched precariously on stacks of equipment. I go to visit a friend of mine in Germany. There I wait anxiously to hear from Schweitzer. He is planning a train trip through Germany and the Netherlands before returning to Africa, and I hope so much that I'll be able to help by driving him to certain villages difficult to reach by rail.

17

WITHIN A FEW WEEKS I got the letter from Dr. Schweitzer I'd been hoping for. It read:

Dear Erica:

Now I have to call on you, if it is possible for you to be at my disposal. I arrive in Heidelberg from Hamburg on Thursday, November 1 at 5:05 p.m. I have to visit friends in Württemberg. The train connections are very bad, and I would lose a day that way. Now my request: Wait for me on the Heidelberg train station on November 1 at 5:05 p.m. Drive me to the place where I have to be, and the next day on to Strasbourg. Should I not arrive at 5:05 p.m., wait in the station restaurant until ten in the evening. Then take a room in a hotel as near to the station as possible. Then wait for me on November 2 from eight in the morning on, again in the station restaurant, until I show up. You help me out greatly. I thank you from my heart and I am happy to see you again. In haste with kind greetings,

Yours,

Albert Schweitzer

From this letter I could see that Schweitzer already used the more familiar "du" form of address with me rather than the formal, impersonal "Sie." This is characteristic of Schweitzer; he does not feel comfortable on the "Sie" basis. He feels that every other human being is a friend, and he wants to show this to the other person as soon as he can. Once he told me how lonely Goethe was in his old age.

"Goethe insisted that people, even his old friends, address him with the formal 'Sie,' and 'your excellency.' But that makes for distance. I make it a habit to replace every old friend who passes on with a new one who becomes my *Dutzfreund*."

"Have I replaced someone near to you?" I asked.

"No," he said, laughing. "You always want a special place."

Anyway, on November 1, I left Düsseldorf for Heidelberg in a heavy rain and fog. I wanted to be there by five in the evening even if Schweitzer did not show up at the time he'd given me. I was especially looking forward to seeing him in Heidelberg. I'd never been to the town before, but my father had studied there for his medical examinations in his youth.

When the 5:05 train puffs in, behind a window of a third-class compartment I see the kind old face smiling at me. But the smile vanishes when I try to pick up his metal suitcase for him.

"No discussions," he says, one of his favorite expressions when he does not want an argument. "Where's the car? Let's get going."

Once we are under way, he apologizes that we will not be able to spend any time in Heidelberg.

"Sorry to disappoint you," he says. "But I have to be with my friends tonight, and it is farther from here than I thought. Also the weather is bad. You mustn't drive fast. And these friends I am visiting are in a bad situation. I hope I can do something for them. I am not even sure that we can drive back through Heidelberg. Do you mind terribly?"

I assure him that I do not.

On the way to Heilbronn, Schweitzer tells me about his recent trips through Sweden, England, and Germany, about the enthusiastic response of new friends and old to his philosophical ideas. His talk is so animated, his voice so youthful, that in the dark of the autumn evening I feel as though I have a very young man next to me who has just returned from his first trip into the world.

I am not sure of the road, and in the darkness it is difficult to read the signs. But it is always Schweitzer who jumps out of the car to seek directions, grabbing the hand of whomever we encounter, and always displaying such a rare combination of politeness, directness, and warmth.

Eventually, I lose my way completely, having taken a wrong turn, and we find ourselves at the top of a vineyard on a narrow path surrounded by bushes. The sky is pitch black by now, and the car slithers to a stop in the soft mud. It won't move backward or forward. Dr. Schweitzer gets out of the car to reconnoiter, and he sinks knee-deep into the mud.

"Don't try to move the car back," he calls out. "There's a ditch."

When I get out, I see to my horror that our predicament looks hopeless; the car is deep in mud and perched precariously between the ditch on one side of the road and a ditch on the other side. I get back behind the wheel, and Schweitzer pushes; the night air is so cold I can see his breath turning to steam. I am scared he will catch cold, but he refuses to get back into the car. He stands there in the cold mud, pushing on the rear bumper for several minutes, while I give gas. But the wheels spin and the car won't budge. Then he says firmly:

"I have to get help."

That means a half hour's walk to the next village, and it's questionable whether he'll find anyone at this hour to come with a tow truck. All this effort after he has traveled for two days and nights on the hard bench of a third-class compartment, with nothing to eat but some bread and cheese since he never goes to the dining car! I plead with him to let me go instead, but he's as stubborn as ever, and goes trudging off, a small flashlight in his hand. Each time he takes a step he has to drag his foot out of the soft, wet ground. I follow him with my eyes. I can hardly bear to see him inching across the valley. The smaller his shape gets in the distance, the unhappier I become.

Then I say a childish, frantic prayer. I try to rock the car gently and, for some mysterious reason, my prayer is answered: with a great groan, the car emerges from the mudbank. Off I drive in pursuit of Dr. Schweitzer and find him in the best of humor. He's been walking for about a quarter of an hour, not at all dismayed.

"The adventures we experience!" he says, when he's safe in the car again. "One must allow life to come up with such accidental situations. It is always they which turn out to have been the most memorable."

How grateful I am for his attitude!

When we reach the next village, a few young men are gathered around a fountain, and one of them responds to Dr. Schweitzer's request to show us the way to his friend's house. Dr. Schweitzer plans to be there overnight and asks one young man if there's an inn nearby where I can stay. He takes us to a combination inn and butcher shop called The White Lamb, which strikes us as singularly appropriate, since the mud covering my legs and most of me has dried into a bleak, white color.

Arrangements are made quickly, and the proprietor and his

wife promise to have my room ready by my return. The inn is small and clean, although the smell of the butchershop downstairs is overpowering and nauseating.

As soon as we are on the road again, Schweitzer starts to question our guide.

"Where do you come from?" he asks.

The young man, who has a pleasant, sad-eyed expression, tells us that he is a refugee from Rumania where he, his wife, and three children had been prisoners of the Russians. He managed to escape with his family and is now trying to find work in Germany. His big wish is to get to America to start a new life. Schweitzer takes his little blue notebook out of his pocket, marks down the name and address of the man, and promises to help him find some employment. We drive through an enchanting strip of woodland, where the road is covered with damp autumn leaves that glisten under the headlights.

"The moon is coming out. It's clearing," says Schweitzer. "It will be beautiful tomorrow, and I will tell you about this particular spot of earth, Württemberg, and of the songs and poems it's inspired."

A half hour later we find the tiny hamlet where Schweitzer is to visit. Again I watch him marching off, carrying his luggage. He even insisted on leaving his flashlight with me in case I should need it during the night at The White Lamb.

During the drive back the Rumanian tells me more of the disappointments he has lived through and of his hope for a new life in America. When we stop at the inn, I give him some money and invite him to have a bite to eat with me. But he tells me he is expected home, so I sit alone, eyed curiously by the proprietor and his wife. "Who is this creature?" they seem to be asking. "She speaks German but has an American car. And who was that kind old gentleman who made arrangements for her?" But I do not respond to their questioning eyes, because Schweitzer has asked me not to reveal his identity unnecessarily or to mention his visit in the neighborhood. After some cold cuts and hot tea, I go straight to bed. Before I can even review the day's adventures, I am sound asleep.

Early in the morning I awake from a ray of sunlight playing on my pillow. I try to scrub off my shoes but soon give up. Anyhow, the car is still so full of mud, it would be wasted effort. The car, in fact, originally black, has been transformed into a mud-caked, khaki-colored monstrosity. I am almost ashamed to pick up the Doctor in it, but on second thought, I decide that the car's condition might serve as a kind of camouflage against autograph hunters and the like. Behind such dirty windows no one would see or expect to find the "Grand Docteur"!

In daylight the road is much easier to follow. I drive through the enchanting landscape and arrive at our meeting place before Dr. Schweitzer. I work at the dirt on my shoes a bit, and while I am bending down, busy at them, Dr. Schweitzer's feet appear next to mine. His shoes are clean and shining, and I wonder how he got them that way. He smiles at me, gets into the car, and we head back for Heilbronn. On the way, Dr. Schweitzer talks in a constant flow about the poet Mörike, who grew up in this part of the world, about art, politics, philosophy, and he grows more exuberant as the sun rises higher and the day brightens. Every well-cared-for field we pass gives him joy, every little cart, every dumpheap. Especially dumpheaps! He explains to me their importance:

"Once when a journalist asked me about civilization, I answered, 'It all begins with the dungheap. If a dungheap is looked after well and built as it should be, you can be sure that the people who built it are civilized.' I'm afraid that journalist did not understand what I meant, but ever since then I say, 'Civilization starts with the dungheap, the *Misthaufen.*'"

We laugh into the sunshine. It feels so much like vacation time for him, a rarity in his schedule. He talks with admiration of those who fight for freedom and truth, and declares suddenly:

"Listen, Erica. We will make a detour. Ever since I was a student I have wanted to visit the birthplace of Melanchthon, the philosopher who was the right hand of Luther, and the founder of the Humanistic Academic High School."

So off we embark on a pilgrimage to Bretten because there a man was born whose thinking Schweitzer respects. While he talks on, the sun shines in his eyes, and like a boy who has taken a day off from school, he says:

"Think of it. No one in the world knows exactly where we are!"

A little girl, braids flying in the wind, is running down the road ahead of us.

"Pull over," he says. "Maybe we can give her a lift." Then to the child: "Hey, you little frog, where are you off to in such a hurry?"

"To the pharmacy," the little one pipes up. "My mother is sick, and I have to get her some medicine."

"To the pharmacy, then," replies Schweitzer. "Get in, and we'll take you there. Tell me, does the druggist give you some licorice when you buy something?"

"No. Never," replies the little girl.

"Then tell him that the old fellow who gave you a lift is a doctor," says Schweitzer. "And that when he was a child, he always got some free candy in a pharmacy. It's a good old custom and should not be abandoned. What do you want to be when you grow up?"

After a slight pause, the small high voice rings out:

"A fashion designer."

" 'Fashion designer,' " Schweitzer says, imitating her high voice. "Tell me," he continues in his own, "do you know how to sew?"

"No. But I can draw beautifully," the child replies.

"That is good," says Schweitzer. "But you must also learn how to sew. That way you will be a better fashion designer later on. And don't make skirts that are too short, do you hear? And the same applies to your hair—leave it long, whatever fashion dictates."

The child with her high voice and blond braids is shy and a wee bit embarrassed. When we let her out of the car, she dips into a deep curtsy, then blushing, runs into the pharmacy.

18

DRIVING THROUGH the small town of Bretten, Schweitzer asks where the museum is located. The first person he stops answers:

"How strange you should ask me. I am the curator of the museum. It is closed today, but if you are especially interested, I will gladly open it up for you."

Schweitzer thanks him and says:

"How lucky we are today that, of all people, we should bump into you."

We stroll through the museum and look at documents, letters, books, and paintings. The curator wants to explain everything, but it is always Schweitzer who knows more details. After an hour, when we walk through the last room, the curator with a searching look in his eyes asks the Doctor to sign the guestbook.

"Now the cat is out of the bag," Schweitzer says, laughing. "I'll sign it. But I don't want to read about it in the newspaper tomorrow."

The curator, looking over the Doctor's shoulder, exclaims:

"I had my suspicions when I first saw your unruly hair. I thought you looked like Dr. Schweitzer. When I heard you talking about Luther and Melanchthon, I was almost convinced. I am very happy you found your way to visit us. What an honor!"

"Don't say that," Schweitzer replies. "What's honor? Say you are pleased. What an experience for me to come! I have always wanted to."

He shakes hands with the curator; we step into the car again and congratulate each other on our lucky day. The late autumn feels just like summer, and the air is very mild.

"Like driving into one's holidays," Schweitzer says. "I am so glad you could pick me up in Heidelberg."

We drive on to Karlsruhe, not on the autobahn, but over small country roads, and inquire at the police station about the address

101 ॐ

of another of Schweitzer's friends. A policeman tells us that the street no longer exists. Schweitzer does not give up, though. According to little clues he remembers, we take this turn and that, and finally arrive at his friend's house. They are much moved to see each other, and I leave them alone together.

We'd originally planned to stop at a restaurant for lunch, but now Schweitzer decides it would be a waste of time. Instead, we buy cheese and bread for a picnic on the road. He has a huge pear, too, a present from the friends he spent the night with. Because we are both so hungry, he cuts some pieces of bread and cheese, and hands them to me to eat while I drive. As we reach a turn in the road, he asks me to stop.

"Here we will sun ourselves a little, what do you say?"

The autumn trees on the meadow look lovely in their colorful garb. It feels good to stretch my legs, and we wander up and down for a few minutes, talking and eating. Then he peels the pear and offers it to me.

"You didn't have to peel it for my sake," I say.

"That reminds me of the story of the Duke and the gardener," says Schweitzer. "The Duke was taking a walk in his orchard when a young gardener boy offered him two pears. The Duke took one and began to eat it with gusto, leaving the other one for the boy. The youngster then took out a penknife and began to peel his pear carefully. 'What are you doing, stupid?' the Duke asked. 'Don't you know a pear tastes always better with its skin?'

" 'I know, your Lordship,' the boy replied. 'I usually like it that way too, but I dropped one of these pears in the dump heap, and I'm not sure which of the two it was.' "

Schweitzer laughs with me. I have never seen him as happy and carefree as this before. But we still must hurry to make all the stops that he wants before returning to Strasbourg. A bit farther on, we see a man walking slowly on the side of the road.

"Pull up," Schweitzer says. "This fellow needs a lift."

"But look how slowly he's going," I say. "He is just strolling along. His hand isn't up. He doesn't want a lift."

All we see of the man is his back. I don't know why, but Schweitzer is very insistent and orders me to stop. When he asks the pedestrian whether he wants a lift, the young man answers hesitatingly:

102 ❧

"Well . . . Yes. I want to go to Freiburg. I've been on the road since eight this morning."

"Why are you walking so far? Don't you have a bicycle?" asks Schweitzer.

"No, I have nothing," the young man answers. "I'm going to Freiburg to enter an order there. At least they will feed me. Nothing means anything to me any more. Life is not worth it."

The Doctor moves over, making room for our new passenger, and starts to talk of those inner things of value in life. He stresses that one must never, out of despair, give up one's freedom. He talks to the young man, who does not believe in anything, of the obstacles and problems which life can bring, even in a religious order; of the futility of blind obedience without faith; of losing the respect of others in case one decides to leave an order and cannot any more. He talks of the need to start anew when in despair, of the courage to try a fresh way of existence. For seven miles Dr. Schweitzer tries to touch something in the young man which still has a glimmer of faith, a spark of hope. I can feel that the young man, although by no means easily convinced, is listening intently. At last he speaks too, slowly, but with less bitterness and self-pity than before.

"Maybe you have something," he says. "Maybe it is not a coincidence that you picked me up. I did not even bother to raise my hand for a lift any more. I was sure that people didn't care, that people are no good. I have no friend—"

Here the Doctor interrupts him.

"You must not expect anything—from others," Dr. Schweitzer says. "It's you yourself of whom you must ask a lot. Only from oneself has one the right to ask for everything or anything. This way it's up to yourself—your own choice. What you get from others remains a present, a gift!"

"Thank you," says the young man when he steps out of the car. "I'll think about what you said. I will take time before I make a decision."

The Doctor looks tired now, and I feel we should probably drive straight home. But he wants to visit another friend of his—a professor of geology who had been exiled by the Nazis and never been reinstated by the French. We drive into the mountains of the Black Forest, where we are informed that the house cannot be reached by car. Schweitzer insists on going the last mile by foot. But the house, when we reach it, is closed.

"They are shopping in the village," a neighbor tells us.

Back to the village and into many stores we go, looking for his friend. Dr. Schweitzer tells a group of children whom we are looking for, and pretty soon they point out the professor and his wife. The couple are amazed when they recognize Schweitzer. It has been twenty years since they've seen one another!

The four of us go to a small inn where Schweitzer listens to the professor's ideas and views, while his wife and I chat together about more mundane matters. Schweitzer makes many notes in his little blue book, and once, turning to us, puts his finger to his mouth.

"Hush, whisper. Grandfather is trying to concentrate."

In the car afterward, Schweitzer tries to explain his friend's theories to me, but it is a lost labor of love. He soon gives up, but promises to show me first hand in nature evidence of the theories they discussed.

Back in Strasbourg I have dinner with him, Mme. Martin, Mlle. Emma, and Ali Silvers. Both nurses have enjoyed a few days' vacation but seem more happy to be reunited with their Grand Docteur. Despite the day's activities, Dr. Schweitzer is not tired, and declaring that much time could be saved by traveling by car, thanks me for having chauffeured him across country.

The doctor's lively sense of humor, familiar to his friends, is seldom caught in photographs because facing a camera does not amuse him.

Dr. Schweitzer's home in Günsbach is just a few hundred yards from the parsonage where he grew up. Whether he is there or not, his home is a center for visitors and for his friends.

Mrs. Helene Schweitzer (center) with her husband and his sister, Mrs. Adele Woyt, in the garden at Günsbach. After his return from Africa the whole village comes to bid welcome.

Dr. Schweitzer's daughter, Rhena, and his grandchildren in his Günsbach garden. The Eckert family, from left to right: Katrine, Christiane, Monique, Rhena's husband Jean, Rhena, Phillip.

The church where Schweitzer learned to play the organ and where his father preached, stands amid the vineyards that surround Günsbach.

There is something deeply and distinctly personal in Dr. Schweitzer's dealings with people. Above, he listens as a neighbor recites a poem she has composed in his honor; below, he advises another to rest because of her heart condition; opposite, he is surrounded by visitors in his garden, and by a troupe of girl campers.

Dr. Schweitzer had said: "I would like to record a whole program . . . in my little church, here on my organ." Jerome Hill and I, top right, were permitted to arrange for the recording of a program on tape at Günsbach. The organ, damaged during World War II, had been rebuilt under Schweitzer's supervision. The sound truck gave him an opportunity to hear the play-back immediately; he listens, opposite.

Dr. Schweitzer in Europe: above, he strolls on a bridge across the Seine shortly before his address to the French Academy which had elected him to membership. Below, an organ grinder expresses his homage to Dr. Schweitzer in Brussels; opposite, being interviewed in Tübingen in the street before his hotel after receiving an honorary degree from the university.

A brief rest
in a third-class
compartment.

Isaak, a Bordeaux ship porter (left), is always on hand to help
Schweitzer load hospital supplies but will accept no tip from "the
Grand Docteur who went out to Africa to help my brothers."

At Sassandra, a port on the Ivory Coast, cargo is unloaded in the morning
mist. Here, a young priest came on board to meet Schweitzer, whose
autobiography had inspired him to dedicate his life to mission work.

Nearing the end of his tenth journey to Africa, Schweitzer disembarks from the *S. S. Foucauld* at Port Gentil with crates of drugs and supplies for the Lambaréné hospital.

The motor launch moves up the Ogowe River nearing the three islands Schweitzer was passing when, in 1915, the three words "reverence for life" first flashed upon his mind.

Schweitzer returns to the people and the work at Lambaréné in the same
vigorous spirit with which he founded his hospital fifty years ago.

Patients and staff sing a tribute on the Grand Docteur's seventy-eighth birthday. Ephé, a leper, one of the first treated at the hospital, gives a moving speech: "Today I come to thank you and tell everybody how you have helped me..."

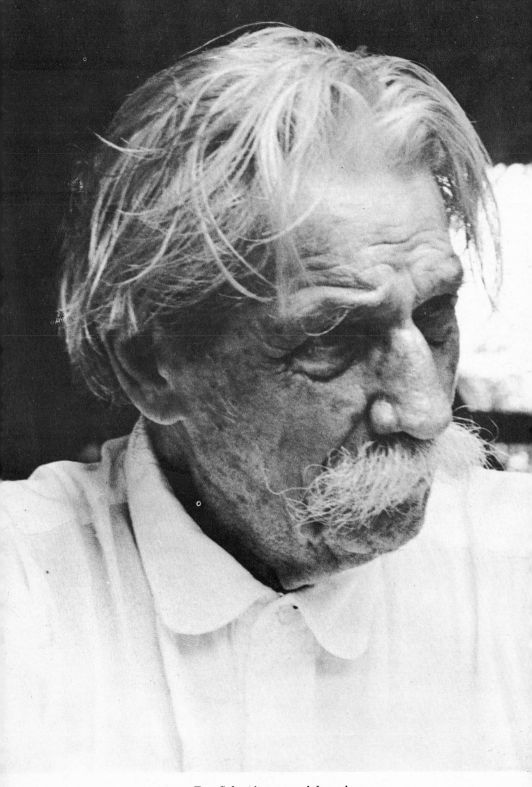

Dr. Schweitzer at eighty-nine.

19

D R. SCHWEITZER's plan is to leave for Bordeaux on November 10 and to sail from there for Africa a few days later. Meanwhile, Jerome Hill has written me:

"Do all you can to convince the Doctor how important it is for us to have shots of his departure in Bordeaux. If possible, travel with him in the train, take pictures of the loading of supplies for Africa. I hope he will consent to this. . . ."

The Doctor does, but not too enthusiastically. Obviously, he will have so much to do, getting ready for the trip, that having me around with my camera can only add to the confusion. But as always, once Dr. Schweitzer accepts the idea, he does so completely, and I have a free hand to photograph the packing of some two hundred cases of instruments, tropical helmets, medicines, and the many other supplies needed at Lambaréné. The packing and crating are enormous physical jobs themselves, and every evening friends of Schweitzer in Strasbourg come over after their regular work to help out. As I watch each case being stamped LAMBARÉNÉ VIA PORT GENTIL, a great homesickness for Africa comes over me, and I wonder if and when I can go there again. I know it cannot be before spring, anyway.

On November 19, I board the train for Bordeaux with Dr. Schweitzer, Mlle. Emma, and Ali Silvers.

To get to Bordeaux fast one can travel today from Strasbourg via Paris and save many hours, but Schweitzer, loyal as he is, likes to take a longer more southerly route, as he did on his first trip to Africa in 1913. To him it means many sights he treasures, and he prefers to remain faithful to them.

We leave from the Colmar station at noon, and among the hundreds seeing him off are a number who have had no chance to visit him during his stay. His heavy metal suitcase and wooden crates have been sent off two days in advance. But he still has quite a bit of hand luggage, which he insists on carrying himself.

Once we are on the open road, settled in our third-class compartment, Schweitzer takes from his old, worn leather satchel a book he wants to read in peace. But by then word has gotten around, as it always does, that he is on board, and many fellow travelers come to chat with him. When it gets dark, he stands alone at the window, at last allowed to think his own thoughts in privacy.

We do not go to the dining car but unpack the food we have brought from Günsbach. With how much affection the packages had been prepared! They contain all the Doctor's favorite snacks: a piece of quiche, an Alsatian cheese cake, a thermos bottle of onion soup, nuts from his walnut tree in the garden, fresh blue plums, a piece of chocolate, and little apples from Alsace.

"From my childhood I am so used to these," he says, munching away. "They'll be the last I'll have for some time."

Mlle. Emma and Ali sit opposite Schweitzer and me. I am excited and happy to be with them. When I see Emma and Ali taking a nap, I hope that Schweitzer will also settle for the night. We have only until two in the morning before changing trains in St. Jean de Fosset. At last Schweitzer moves into a corner and leans his head against his rolled-up Loden coat. I watch his face, sometimes in the dark, then for seconds illuminated by the moonlight shining through the train window. What a powerful face he has, the shock of hair not yet white falling over his forehead. The profile is strong and firm. His eyes are closed, and he breathes very evenly.

An hour before changing trains Schweitzer wakes up and proceeds to take all our luggage down from the racks. He refuses any help, even from Emma, a great organizer herself.

"I am the man in the household," he insists, "and in a battle there should be only one general."

When we change trains, there are no porters anywhere, and Schweitzer handles the whole shift-over across the tracks.

On the second train none of us sleep, and we pull into Bordeaux at seven in the morning. Dozens of reporters await Schweitzer at the station, and they help us move our baggage to the Hotel Commercial across the street. Schweitzer is a past master in involving reporters in some project. Once he had them carry a bed from the third floor to the ground floor for a woman suffering from a heart condition. They always seem to like to be able to assist him.

At the hotel Dr. Schweitzer's room and Emma's are on the ground floor. Ali's and mine are on the third floor, where we are soon joined by Toni van Leer, the Dutch nurse making the trip to Lambaréné with us. The hotel (which has since been renovated) is a typical third-class French establishment with small dingy rooms. But the French windows have lace curtains and look out on a large square in front of the station. A huge clock hangs over the station entrance, and Schweitzer, after moving his writing table to the window, often glances out and says: "Hurry! It's time to finish our last letters from Europe."

Even in Bordeaux many friends join us for meals at the hotel, and the Doctor's writing schedule is continually interrupted. He works at his correspondence right after waking up, and whenever we come to pick him up for breakfast at eight o'clock, he has already finished a few letters. There is much last-minute shopping to be done, many errands, and always lunch with friends; in the afternoon, no siesta, but a trip to the docks to supervise the loading of cases and boxes. After more letter writing, dinner at seven.

I am happy that I am not just in the way, taking pictures, but can help out with the correspondence. Schweitzer has been elected a member of the French Academy, and each of the forty different members has invited him to accept and attend a meeting. In his typical way, he insists that each one be answered! I type every evening after dinner. Around eleven o'clock he tells me to stop work. But when I inquire the next morning what time he went to bed himself, he answers: "Never ask. Your question is a sign that you don't know me well. Never ask me how I feel or what time I went to bed." But Mlle. Emma confides to me: "His light stayed on until two this morning."

The day of his departure comes. We leave the hotel right after breakfast. Stacks of letters have arrived in the morning mail, and as soon as Schweitzer is installed in his cabin on board ship, he proceeds to answer what he terms his "very last letters from Europe."

Then, when it is time to say good-by, no words will come to me. But he understands my silence. I try hard to keep my emotion back until it is time for me to photograph the ship edging out of the pier. I have my cameras set up on the top of a building across from the boat. Through my tears I cannot even gauge the distance correctly. (When we watched these films later, they were hopelessly out of focus.) In the end I abandon my camera and run alongside the slowly moving ship, until it reaches the end of the docks and starts down the river.

20

B ACK IN NEW YORK, I received a letter from Schweitzer even more encouraging than the one he'd sent me after my first return from Africa. By now he was interested in the film project, and referred to it as "our film," surely a good omen. The months in New York went by fast. Jerome edited the organ recordings and we assembled the film material. We had no definite continuity in mind yet, because we still had no interior shots of the hospital. They would come on my next trip, when I'd have generators, lights, and cables with me. Jerome was so encouraged by Dr. Schweitzer's interest in doing the organ recordings that he sent him a beautiful record player for his birthday on January 14, 1952. In reply, Schweitzer suggested that I come back to Africa in March—the beginning of the dry season in Lambaréné. By that time, he explained, the building of the new leper village would have started, and he'd be working out of doors much of the time. Not only that. He'd be going back to Alsace for a visit later in the summer, where we could work more on that part of the film, as well as finish up the organ recordings.

When I land again on the Lambaréné airstrip on March 17, I am deeply touched at the warm greetings of the lepers waiting in the pirogue to paddle me to the hospital. One of them, Obiange, grins and says:

"The Grand Docteur told us to sing loudly when the boat draws near the hospital, so he is sure to come down to the river to welcome you."

When the roofs of the hospital appear, and the oarsmen start to row with extra swiftness, I can see many white figures gathering at the landing. Schweitzer is already waving a huge white handkerchief. When I land, he holds out his hand, saying:

"Welcome back to Africa."

I am housed in the same room I shared with Julia on the first trip. *Sans Souci,* the staff and visitors' building, is being enlarged and the new rooms will hopefully be ready in two weeks. In fact, the whole of Lambaréné is in a tumult of expansion and reconstruction. There is so much enthusiasm in the air, it seems to me as if Schweitzer is just starting his African career. In addition to the new leper village, the hospital itself is being enlarged to make room for the increase in patients. The miraculous results of the new antibiotics and other drugs has made the natives flock there from over two hundred miles in every direction. And, of course, the lepers as well as the other patients bring their families with them.

At the construction site of the leper village the next morning, I have never seen Schweitzer so full of energy as he works. When I ask Monenzali, the carpenter, how often the Doctor comes out there, he replies:

"Oh, just once a day. But he stays all day."

It is true. Schweitzer leaves right after breakfast with the most able of his crew. He clears the jungle, fells trees, extracts rocks from the terrain, climbs ladders, measures planks, in addition to supervising the whole operation. It is really wonderful to watch him for hours on end under the brilliant sun, sweating and often shouting at the slow pace of his helpers. Without his active presence, it seems obvious that no work could go on. It needs his firm words of encouragement, his smiles and jokes, just to keep the crew in a functioning mood.

He allows me to come with him, often from early in the morning until late in the evening. I shoot thousands of feet of film—this time, I hope, with good results. I am lucky to find in Dr. Percy a skillful electrician who hooks up cables to the two generators I have brought with me. With his help, and everyone else's, I get a faithful record of the work inside the hospital, too. But the technical difficulties Schweitzer cited in his first letter to me have not been exaggerated. Also, the natives who do not know me well continue either to stare into the camera or to run away from it. I feel quite a sense of victory when Camille (whom Dr. Schweitzer calls "Puss in Boots" because of his huge black leather shoes of Chaplinesque proportions) says to me:

"Is the Doctor not happy with you? Why do you leave after a few months when the others stay for years?"

He has taken me for one of the staff, only that I, instead of administering drugs or treating the patients, work with a camera!

When the weather is too bad for taking pictures, I pitch in with other work, too. I carry wood to the building site, water from the river, and try to supervise the workers when Schweitzer is called away on other duties. In all honesty, though, I must confess that I am a complete flop in the role of supervisor. The natives are friendly enough with me, but neither firmness nor pleading can make them take my authority seriously. No matter how often Schweitzer tells them to respect my orders, as though they were his, it does not work; they will either meander along at their usual minimum pace, or wander off altogether.

They give me the nickname of *Madame Cinéma*, and after Schweitzer has left me alone with them for a while, one of them will start the exodus rolling by coming over and saying, *"Madame Cinéma, j'ai besoin!"* This is their way of asking permission to disappear behind the bushes for a few minutes; but once they've gotten out of my sight, they never come back—at least not until they see or hear Schweitzer in the distance. To keep them vaguely under my sway, I try bribery, stuffing the pockets of my nurse's uniform full of candy. When the work begins to lag, I walk around encouragingly, handing out the sweets. It works—until my pockets are empty.

As far as the film is concerned, the actual photography is going so well that I hate to bother Schweitzer about production plans, but Jerome Hill insists that I find out who Schweitzer thinks would be the best script writer.

"Would you approve of Thornton Wilder?" I ask him one day on the way to lunch.

"Listen, Erica," he replies, as though he's just been considering the same problem himself. "There is only one man who can write this story."

"Who is that?" I ask.

"Myself," he replies.

"What?" I ask, flabbergasted. "I could not allow you to undertake this, now that I know you better, now that I can see the enormous amount of your daily work. Besides, you'll have to read and approve the script anyway. That will be bad enough. But writing the complete film script—that is a different kind of matter, very complicated and nerve-wracking. Don't even consider it. Let me contact Wilder, and see what he has to say."

"You are a fine one," he replies, frowning. "First you thread the needle, you get the ball rolling, and then when I co-operate with you, you want to dictate the terms. Nothing doing. Either I write the script, or there's no script at all."

And that is it. Of course he is right in one sense. His story can best be told by him. But when will he really have the time? It is this factor that makes me wonder if Jerome will consent to the idea. While these doubts are bothering me, Schweitzer proceeds to write Jerome himself. He repeats in the letter that he does not want the film shown before his death and that he will write the script whenever possible. He adds that since he expects to be around a few more years, there should be no great hurry. And since the three of us have agreed to this principle already, there should be no problem, even if it is a couple of years before he settles down to write it.

Jerome, in his reply, agrees, but expresses politely the hope that Schweitzer can get around to doing the script soon. He also feels that more can be said about the recognition Schweitzer has gained in the world if at least part of the script is written by an objective outsider.

Every day Schweitzer is the first one up, the last to bed. On the construction site, in the hospital, at his desk, on the scaffolding of the new buildings, he is untiringly at work. It is still he who orders the drugs, who diagnoses every difficult case, who settles "palavers" among the people and, whenever necessary, among the staff. But, perhaps because I am so bad at it myself, I most enjoy watching the way he handles his helpers. After he works with them for an hour, he gives them a ten-minute rest period. When he claps his hands and calls *"Répos"* they answer: *"Merci, Docteur."* They shout out the two words always in a joyous chorus because they are so looking forward to the rest period.

Sometimes Schweitzer sits down, too, and pulls out his handkerchief to make a seat for me next to him on a tree trunk or a packing case. During these pauses he likes to talk about his other concerns: his unfinished books, *The Kingdom of God* and the third volume of *The Philosophy of Civilization* . . . his interpretation of the Bach trills . . . the problems at the hospital . . . the shipment of rice or wood that has not shown up yet . . . the new doctor that is expected . . . the protocol that must be followed on the trip from Bordeaux to Port Gentil, what should be worn, what injections must be taken . . . an unlimited variety of obligations to be fulfilled.

When the ten minutes are up, though, Schweitzer rises and shouts: *"Au travail!"* Then the workers pick up their tools slowly and resume work.

One day after the rest period is over and Schweitzer has shouted *"Au travail!"* Simon, a youngster, yells out: *"Merci, Docteur!"*

"Are you crazy?" the grownup co-workers ask. "To say thank you when you have to go *back* to work?"

Schweitzer has a good laugh at the youngster, but then he adds seriously, patting his head:

"You have a big secret, whether you know it or not. The secret of enjoying your work. It is a great wisdom, my boy. Hang on to it."

21

THIS TIME when I left Lambaréné, the film was well under way, and our plans were definite for meeting in Europe again later in the summer. In New York, in the screening room day after day, it was a joy to watch all the footage I'd taken gradually acquiring shape. The atmosphere of the hot, steaming jungle came across, the sad eyes of the suffering patients, the young children frolicking in the river. But we still didn't have a single word of accompanying script, only some recordings of jungle and hospital sounds—the early morning bell, the singing of the natives, Schweitzer's voice calling out a command or encouragement. Jerome, in fact, was quite worried about the script. He felt that Schweitzer, in writing it, could not and would not touch on what he meant to his patients, his staff, and the outside world.

"I don't think he's aware of his own importance," Jerome said. "Also, he would be much too modest to talk about this. It will need an outsider. Write to Wilder and let's hear what he says."

Because I could not conceive of Schweitzer ever having time to do it all alone, I consented. But within a few days Thornton Wilder answered, expressing enthusiasm for the project, but regretting that his commitment to his own writing would prevent him from helping us.

In addition to Wilder's letter, we suffered another setback. A film company in France approached Schweitzer with the idea of doing a dramatization of certain parts of his life by a young French playwright. Schweitzer agreed. Although it was to be a theatrical film, quite different in treatment from our documentary, I couldn't help wondering how it would affect our eventual success.

A group of ten actors and cameramen went to Lambaréné "just for background shots." When the script was finished, Schweitzer penciled in corrections and gave them help, as he always does. The result was a great deal of publicity in the papers about Schweitzer's interest in the project. Jerome did not think this changed our position, but I was horribly jealous. Their film *Il est Minuit Docteur* was practically finished already in a burst of publicity, whereas we had been denied permission to release the film, even when it was completed. The slow and solid building of our work seemed to me undermined. But when I wrote to Dr. Schweitzer of my worries, he answered:

"Oh ye of little faith! Have I not promised to co-operate with you? Their film is just theater. The French government is interested in furthering one of their young playwrights. I cannot and will not hamper his chances. But our film is real. It is we who must proceed slowly and do our best. Has not that always been our principle?"

We are all together again in Günsbach in July. Schweitzer has arrived in wonderful spirits, eager to record the huge program of Bach, Widor, Mendelssohn, and César Franck. And he keeps his promise to himself to play the entire program by heart. We have to close the church while recordings are being taken, but during the many hours of rehearsal the church is always filled with friends and visitors. And outside, the neighbors go about their work, harvesting their fields while the music sounds through the valley.

The film material covering Schweitzer's boyhood in Günsbach is shaping up well. Dr. Schweitzer's grandson enacts scenes from the Doctor's boyhood most convincingly, and Dr. Schweitzer's sister, who bears a strong resemblance to their mother, performs in one scene too.

Schweitzer's plan is to return to Africa in early December. I explain to him and Jerome how important it will be for the film for me to accompany him on at least one voyage. Schweitzer agrees, but Jerome does not. He feels that we have so much material to compress into the Doctor's life story that to linger on a seventeen-day ocean trip will be a waste of time and money. He wants to sum up the trip with a mere diagram on a map. I get stubborn.

"Give me a leave of absence," I plead. "I will finance this portion of the film myself if the material I get is not used. If it is, so much the better. Either way, it's my gamble."

Jerome finally agrees, and Dr. Schweitzer and I embark for

Lambaréné aboard his favorite ship, *Le Foucauld*. When the ship leaves the quai, it glides alongside the forest of cranes, then enters the Garonne, which flows toward the Gironde. The river's edge shines with bright autumn colors, and soon the light rain we've set sail under gives way to a mild evening sunshine. Schweitzer wears the old hat he's worn so many times on this voyage. He cannot bear to give it up, despite the many offerings from friends of a new one. During the night we slip through the dangerous sandbanks at the mouth of the Gironde into the bay of Biscay, where we run into a storm that keeps up for three days. When it stops, we move swiftly south, in plain sunshine. The weather grows quickly warmer, and Dr. Schweitzer's khaki suit replaces the dark Loden coat he always wears in Europe. He soon has to put away the old hat, too, for his tropical sun helmet.

We pass Las Palmas, the most beautiful of the Canary Islands, in the early evening. Then night comes. By the next morning we are sailing along the rocky white coast of Mauretania, Cape Blanc glistening in the sun.

Dr. Schweitzer has introduced me to the captain, who gives me permission to roam around freely on board, taking pictures. But I am distressed that Dr. Schweitzer does not spend more time on deck. He said before sailing that he was looking forward to the trip for a good rest. But once on board, he has spent practically all day in his cabin, writing letters. While I am filming the many native women on board luxuriating under the modern hair dryers of the ship's beauty shop, the coiffeur confides to me:

"After myself, I think that Dr. Schweitzer is the busiest man on board."

Each day at breakfast I implore the Doctor to spend more time on deck.

"Why don't you ever take a siesta?" I ask. "Why don't you walk around?"

But he replies:

"I have to answer at least one fifth of the letters I have with me. I have to give instructions by mail for an organ being built in Switzerland by an American friend. I have to write in detail to the new doctor who is joining us in Lambaréné. If you need me for some important filming up on deck, I am at your service. But do not add to my worries. Undisturbed writing is my relaxation."

(Out of curiosity I roughly clocked the amount of time Dr. Schweitzer spent on deck: during the entire seventeen-day voyage, twenty-seven minutes!)

On the sixth day as we near Cape Verde, the stony coastline changes to green. We swing around the cape in a loop to reach the harbor island of Dakar. Here I want to take pictures, so I ask Dr. Schweitzer to come with me. He dons his helmet, and we climb to the upper deck, where he tells me about Gorée Island.

"Slave dealers settled here in the seventeenth and eighteenth centuries," he says. "They didn't dare settle on the coast itself, where the indigènes might have killed them. But on the island they felt more secure and built it up into a kind of fortress. Their prisoners were incarcerated in the cellars of the fortress and then sold as slaves. Payment consisted of liquor, tobacco, lead, copper, guns, cooking pots, axes, and other tools. Even today one can still see the iron rings onto which the prisoners were chained by the neck. Thousands of them died. When I came here on my first trip to Lambaréné, the harbor of Dakar was still being built. It has great importance. The ships that travel between Europe and South America, as well as those that work along the African coast, all put in here. They stop to trade, as well as to replenish their supplies of coal and oil."

When we dock, the traffic up and down the gangplank is as hectic as that on the escalator of a New York department store. The natives are quite tall, and the women wear heavy gold jewelry in their ears and sometimes small ornaments in their noses. Their luggage consists of unwieldy, untidy bundles, and babies are slung about their shoulders. The chatter is loud and happy.

For the natives who board the ship at Dakar, huge canvas awnings are strung up on the fore and aft decks to protect them from the sun and rain. The scene resembles a native village in miniature.

"Most of these passengers are on their way to trade their wares down the coast," Schweitzer explains to me. "They travel a lot these days and they don't go home until their valuables are sold. Basically they're not too different from your traveling salesmen in America. They peddle anything from carved figurines to modern combs, mirrors, and shoelaces. Even those who are just visiting relatives along the coast carry things to sell and pay for expenses. On their return trip, they'll take back a few things to sell at home. Traveling is expensive in Africa, too."

Walking through the encampment, Schweitzer starts up conversations with many of the travelers; he is recognized and welcomed by some who have been treated at his hospital.

Several Catholic missionaries are on the boat, who seek Schweitzer out and question him about his experiences in the jungle. With those who are on their first trip, Schweitzer is especially sympathetic, giving them specific suggestions with great patience and care.

When we dock at Sassandra, a young Alsatian missionary comes on board to visit Dr. Schweitzer. While he was a prisoner of the Russians during the war, Dr. Schweitzer's autobiography had been loaned to him by another prisoner. After reading it, he vowed that should he ever escape or be freed, he would become a missionary and work in Africa, too. Dr. Schweitzer spends the entire time at Sassandra with the young man who never expected to meet the one whose life so influenced his own.

At Sassandra, which is a very small harbor town on the coast, about forty natives come on board to load and unload freight. Some of them reach the deck by shinnying up ropes. Others are hoisted across on a box resembling a small merry-go-round in an amusement park. The order that only four men can travel in the box each trip is completely ignored, and twenty or more cling to it for the precarious journey. To my chagrin, Schweitzer will not permit me to make the trip with them to get pictures. Pointing to the tattered rope, he says:

"What would I tell Jerome if you were disabled, even in the line of duty? Nothing doing."

Actually, it does look pretty risky, so I obey.

From Sassandra on, good harbors are few along the coast, and the ship often has to tie up at floats, from which freight is towed into shore on huge barges. For carrying passengers to and from the ship, the same odd box is used. Even in good weather the water is too rough for any other method to work. Under such conditions, the hoisting and lowering of the box requires considerable skill, and the native crews are specially trained for the job; they take orders only from their own boss, never from the ship's officers. I love these stops when I can photograph the merry-go-round box, sometimes filled to the brim with an entire family and their belongings; as it swings through the air to land safely, but none too gently, the children let out delighted shrieks, as if they were riding a roller coaster.

In the evenings, before I go to bed, Schweitzer usually reads me a few passages from the Bible that he's given me. It is the hour of the day I look forward to most. Any questions I ask about the text, no matter how minor, he answers with the greatest patience. One night, though, a most embarrassing thing happens: in the midst of Schweitzer's reading, I fall asleep. I am really ashamed. Here is the hour with him I cherish the most, and I, like a school-girl, conk out completely. In fact, it is just like my schooldays when I'd fall asleep as my father was coaching me in Latin. But, unlike my father, Schweitzer simply sends me off to bed, reassuring me that "if I had to run around all day with a camera, I'd be tired, too." This from Schweitzer, who scarcely seems to need sleep at all!

For several days the ship keeps close to the wooded coastline until we reach the large lagoon just outside of Abidjan, an important trading center on the Ivory Coast. Two rafts pull up to each side of the ship, and small motor boats transport passengers and freight across to land.

Dr. Schweitzer and I climb down to one of the rafts. I then take pictures of him engaged in animated conversation with the ship's cook who is looking out from a porthole. I have my cameras set up to take pictures of the boats loaded with native women in colorful garbs, but, just when I am about to start shooting, Schweitzer suddenly grabs me with one hand, my tripod and camera with the other.

"What are you doing?" I cry out. And just as he gives me a great shove, disregarding my protests, a heavy box filled with tin cans crashes down on the very spot where I've been standing. I am stupefied. "Did you see the box falling?" I asked the Doctor.

"No," he says wonderingly. "That was the strange thing about it. I just had the feeling that you were in danger. I didn't see anything."

Many times later he would refer to this incident and insist that my devotion to him stemmed from it. "Like the Czarina was devoted to Rasputin," he would joke.

In Lomé, our next port of call, the sun is shining brilliantly.

All around us small tugboats rock on the waves. This time Protestant missionaries come to visit Dr. Schweitzer. He listens to their problems, then entertains them with anecdotes and episodes from his life at the Lambaréné hospital.

In the afternoon I translate into English for Dr. Schweitzer a letter to the American who is building an organ in a small village in Switzerland. It is a fifteen-page letter—and gives exact specifications about stops, tone quality, and voices for the new organ. No detail is left out. The organ builder will not make a mistake if he follows these loving instructions.

At sunset on the sixteenth day on board ship, as a red glow steals into the cabin and Dr. Schweitzer notices me peering out the porthole, he says:

"Run up. Perhaps you'll get some good shots now. These sunsets near the equator are beautiful and unique because of the mist and a special formation of clouds. I'll join you in a few minutes, if I can. But hurry! The sun sinks fast."

I make it just in time for a few good shots of the sunset, but Schweitzer remains in his cabin.

When we disembark the next day at Port Gentil, at the mouth of the Ogowe River, word has gotten around that the Doctor is in town, and for breakfast we already have a company of twelve. Schweitzer catches up with news of his friends there and talks animatedly about his weeks in Europe. Dr. and Mrs. Ladislaus Goldschmidt, who had worked in Lambaréné for several years as doctor and nurse, invite us for lunch. We are picked up later and driven back by the owner of a gold mine in the Gabon, a former patient of Dr. Schweitzer's. On the way we stop to watch the huge tree trunks floating in the bay, waiting for shipment to Europe and America.

"The red okoumé trees are cut in the Ogowe region," the Doctor explains. "The wood is excellent for peeling off in thin layers and is used all over the world in high-grade plywood. The trunks are towed down the Ogowe, then stored in small bays here, ready for loading. These artificial bays are made by tying several tree trunks together with wire ropes. But unfortunately, the trees do not always stay together like good sheep. In a bad wind or storm, they jump over each other, and many trees float out to sea. Usually, though, they are carried back into harbor by a high tide."

Dr. Schweitzer points at some natives who are standing bare-footed on the huge trees, prodding at them with long sticks. "See how they guide them back in line again!" In the far distance we see many freighters waiting. Tugboats are hurrying toward them, the tree trunks in tow.

At the Port Gentil warehouse where we pass through customs in the afternoon, Dr. Schweitzer proudly displays beautifully executed lists on which he has spent many hours, marking down each item with its original value translated into equatorial money. Every crate is opened again, the contents checked, and the value confirmed. It is terribly tedious work. Fortunately, the customs people, knowing from long experience how orderly he is, help him complete the inspection so that we can return to the Protestant mission station by sundown.

When we arrive at the mission to spend the night, Dr. Schweitzer's old friend, M. Perron, offers to give us a lift up the river to Lambaréné on his motor launch. This means that we won't have to wait for the regular river steamer. The trip will take two days, and I look forward to every minute of it.

"You're certainly a lucky girl," Schweitzer says to me. "You'll get much better pictures this way than on the steamer."

Early the next morning as we start out, the sky looks quite threatening.

"I hope we can make it from the bay into the river before the storm starts," Schweitzer says. "The ocean can be quite rough, and I don't want you to be seasick—for our sake as well as yours!"

Besides the Doctor, M. Perron, and myself, the boat carries Mlle. Kottman, who has come up to Port Gentil to meet us, and a former nurse at the hospital whom we are dropping off on the way. Her husband owns fish hatcheries upriver. Schweitzer tells me where to put up my cameras to get the best shots and plants himself next to me, half sitting on the edge of the railing and watching the clouds overhead. We cross the bay of Port Gentil in about an hour and a half.

"We had to start our trip at high tide," Schweitzer tells me. "Only then is the water high enough to get us over the sandbanks into the mouth of the Ogowe."

A small blinking light points the way toward the river mouth. It runs through mangrove bushes, which appear to be growing right out of the ocean. It begins to get lighter as we reach a small arm of the Ogowe. We travel along it for many hours, on each side of us nothing but thickly clustered mangroves. Dr. Schweitzer arranges himself on a wooden crate, holds on his lap a piece of cardboard, and spreads some writing paper out on another crate in front of him. On and off his eyes glance over the Ogowe. He seems pleased to be undisturbed and able to work on his writing.

I stay close to my camera. Slowly the mangroves are replaced by pandamus trees. Neither variety requires firm earth, and their roots grow in water covered with mud. Until we see trees of more ordinary character, we know that there is no firm land around us.

The little launch has a comfortable cabin space below deck, where Mlle. Kottman prepares a simple but delicious lunch. M. Perron studies the map, while native boys take turns at the wheel. After lunch we all stretch out for siestas, wherever we are, and, by three in the afternoon, we enter a wider arm of the river. Several times we have to cross from one side of the water to the other so as not to get stuck on waterlogged trees lying on sandbanks just below the water's surface. The late autumn rainy season is almost over, and the waters are not very high, though no sandbanks are visible yet.

In the middle of the afternoon we dock at the home of the nurse whose husband owns the fish hatcheries. He welcomes us warmly, and we stay half an hour in their cozy cottage on the water before we are off again. As I film the beautiful crown of a white blooming kapok tree, Schweitzer settles down beside me.

"In this landscape so many memories of former trips run through my mind," he says. "Especially vivid is the river trip of 1929 when on Christmas day I wrote the preface to the *Mysticism of Paul the Apostle*. The last chapter of the book I'd finished during the ocean voyage from Bordeaux."

We still pass no villages, just an occasional canoe paddled by women or children. It is very peaceful. The sun sets fast, and we, on deck, enjoy the light breeze and the last glows of daylight playing on the water. When it grows completely dark, we cast anchor. The pilot says he is just too tired to take us farther upstream by night. The constant watching for sandbanks is especially trying. We sit up all night watching the tropical sky heavy with glistening stars. Venus settles over the golden sickle of the moon, and we admire the spectacle.

The next morning we reach a village where Dr. Schweitzer tells me to get my cameras set up.

"This is the village of Igendja," he explains. "Soon we will come to the three islands I was passing in 1915 when the idea first came to me that *reverence for life* is the basic principle of ethics and true humanity."

I take pictures of him looking out over the three islands.

"If this were the dry season, we'd have great trouble passing these islands," the Doctor says. "Rhinos or hippos would be playing here, just as they were when those three words flashed upon my mind."

Later we pass other villages whose inhabitants rush toward the river edge to wave and shout at their "Grand Docteur"—all friends or patients of his. And soon the hospital's landing place is in sight. There is much excitement there. Doctors, nurses, orderlies, patients, dogs, cats, sheep, goats, pelicans, storks—all are waiting for him. The Lambaréné hospital without Dr. Schweitzer is like an orphanage. Now their father is returning. They all want to show him what it means to them to have him back.

"Home again in Africa," says Schweitzer, stepping on land.

22

M Y STAY in Lambaréné is to be for just a few weeks this time—long enough to be with Dr. Schweitzer on his seventy-eighth birthday.

The ocean voyage seems to have done him much good, even though he stayed in his cabin writing through most of the trip. He plunges right into his most urgent hospital duties, and after catching up, sets aside one hour each evening to work with me on the film script. We decide to follow the pattern of an actual day in Lambaréné, and he begins sketching out the text. It is hard and unfamiliar work for him.

On Saturday evenings we sometimes play the recordings the Doctor has done in Günsbach. Dr. Percy hooks up the record player to the electric generator I've brought for my indoor shots. It works well and it is a new experience for Dr. Schweitzer and his staff that one can hear a concert right here in Lambaréné.

Four days before Dr. Schweitzer's birthday, there is much secret activity around the hospital. Everyone is working on some little present for him, the native workers as well as the staff members and patients. One day I see some children gathering mangoes on the hospital plantation, and when I ask them if they like the fruit, they reply:

"This is not for us. It is for the Grand Docteur on his birthday!"

On the morning of the 14th of January I get up earlier than usual. Everyone else seems to have the same idea. They are rushing in and out of the dining room, carrying leaves and wild flowers from the jungle. Several nurses put down a garland to decorate the table. One nurse has painted a lovely jungle landscape on a native-style mat to which we all sign our names. A crowd of natives gather in front of the Doctor's room, and doctors and nurses come from all directions. I have brought a new photograph of Dr. Schweitzer's favorite wild pig, Thekla, and her small companion, Isabelle. I join the crowd. When everybody is assembled, Mlle. Emma and Mlle. Kottman come from their rooms. Emma gives the sign, and we all begin to sing. When the Grand Docteur opens his door he stands there, listening, his head slightly bowed. He looks so much younger than his years in his white suit, his eyes fresh and rested. When the song is over he says quietly:

"Merci tout le monde et bon jour."

Each person walks up to shake his hand and congratulate him. In the dining room Dr. Percy has put on a new record that Jerome Hill has sent. It is a recording of the whistle the little train sounds when reaching and leaving the Günsbach station, and, on the reverse side, of the bells chiming from the churches of the Münster Valley. Schweitzer cocks his head and suddenly smiles in recognition.

"Why that's the ten o'clock train on Sunday morning!" he exclaims. "Imagine that!"

When the coffee has been poured, Dr. Schweitzer opens each little package, thanks everyone individually, and laughs out loud at some funny animals one of the nurses has carved in wood for him. When breakfast is almost over, a choir of young voices starts outside the dining room, boys from the mission school who have come to sing for the Doctor. He rises at once and walks into the midst of the youngsters, listening with bowed head.

Then a latecomer arrives to bring him a present—an old native who has suffered from leprosy for years. He says that his gift consists of only a few words but that he'd like everyone present to hear them. Ephé is his name. He stands up in front of Dr. Schweitzer and begins:

"Grand Docteur, today I want to thank you and tell everybody how you have helped me. I am only one among many. One cannot count them, so give me your ear and listen to what I have to say. It was in 1913 that we learned that you would come to us, to care for us as a doctor. I, Ephé, was still quite a young man then. I'd prepared myself to become a preacher. Since 1910 I'd known that I was a leper. It was that year that I first saw the spots, red ones, on my body. That made me very sad. I came to you and you gave yourself great pain with me. You gave me the oil of chaulmoogra and it helped me. There was a great improvement in my disease, not only because of the oil, but because you shared with me my sorrow. You treated me like your sick brother, and my heart was made much lighter. I walked from village to village and preached, and I told the listeners that the Grand Docteur was our brother, who had come to stay with us to help us against the terrible disease to which we fall prey. But in later years, when the war took you away from us, my illness became worse again. I often thought of you and thought wonderingly whether God would send you back to us. I prayed for it, for your return, Grand Docteur, but my illness became worse and worse. My hands became deformed. I lost weight. I had the fever and great sores opened up on my feet. One day when I had almost lost hope, I heard you had come back. I begged my brothers to carry me to you. 'Ephé,' you said. 'Ephé, my friend, here I am to help you again.'

"You built me a hut for myself because no one else could share my place with me. The stink of my sores was unbearable, even to me. You came every day. You washed my wounds. You bandaged them. You gave much time and patience to me. Only with those who are well and who don't want to work do you grumble loudly. One day you said to me, 'Now, Ephé, I will give you a new American medication against leprosy. The pus will stop running. Your sores will close. Your poor body will heal again. You will be able to walk again. You will be able to preach again your catechism in the villages.'

"That was how you spoke and how it happened. First I was able to sleep again because the suffering was less. The pain was not so terrible any more. Then the pus stopped running. After three months, I was healed. And now today I can march from one village to another. I always come back to you to show myself, as you told me to. But on your birthday I come not because I want to show myself at the hospital. I come because I want to see you. I want you to know that I pray to the Lord that he keeps you here because we not only need you. We love you."

So speaks Ephé, his hands maimed, his body thin, but his eyes glowing with gratitude. Dr. Schweitzer puts his arm around him.

"I thank you for coming on my birthday," he tells him. "Yes, you and I, we grew old together. We belong together."

EPILOGUE

IT TOOK FIVE MORE YEARS before the film was completed. During those years it was my privilege to be able to return to Lambaréné to film the ongoing work there and also to accompany Dr. Schweitzer on his three trips to Europe, where he appreciated my chauffeuring more than he had my incessant picture taking.

Schweitzer finally consented to the film's release. What made him change his previously stanch position was the trend toward larger screens that started in the late fifties and which threatened, if we waited too many years, to make our film technically obsolete. Although the film was very generously received by the critics and the general public (it won the Academy Award "Oscar" as the best documentary of 1958), Dr. Schweitzer did not see it himself until his last visit to Europe in the summer of 1959 when a special showing was arranged in Münster.

A few days before the showing, Schweitzer is scheduled to give a short talk to a meeting of Swiss and Alsatian helpers on their way to Lambaréné. He tries to sum up some of the problems that he now has to contend with. Following an introduction by a former co-worker, Dr. Trenscz, Schweitzer speaks extemporaneously in his native Alsatian dialect:

"I see already some cigarettes flickering. Most of you have finished your coffee, so now you can listen to me. Those who are not quite finished can go ahead with their food. It will not hurt my speech, they can pay attention anyway.

"You have been told about the 'middle ages' of the hospital by my former colleague, Dr. Trenscz. He told most of the story but not all, so I have to add a few things. First of all, Dr. Trenscz himself played a big part in the construction of the hospital. When we were worried about how to arrange the rooms in the main building, I had a different idea from Trenscz, but he interfered and in the end I took his advice about how and where to place the operating room and maternity ward. Many times, even today, when I walk through the hospital, I think that if I had not followed his advice, I might not have such a well-organized main building. This is the truth. So about the middle ages you have been informed pretty well. Now comes the new era —modern times. In history, every schoolboy can tell when modern times started; in regard to the hospital I, too, can determine this pretty accurately.

"Modern times at the hospital started in the year 1958. I will tell you how. The year before I had made a vow that no one would ever persuade me to build again. We had enough space and did not need any new buildings. I really thought that I was old enough to say sincerely: 'I will not build any more. I have no one to help me with such things anyway. Therefore, all that's finished.' This was a nice thought for me, but it worked out differently, because very strange things happened.

"I first had to face the fact that we needed some space to store petroleum for our generators, and it had to be stored a good distance from living quarters in case it should be struck by lightning and start a fire. So I decided to build near the garden, away from our houses, a room where we would store oil and petrol.

"But I said to myself: 'This is only a little diversion. My vow of not building still holds.' So I was getting set to start that when something else happened. An engineer from Zurich offered to build me a house, a prefabricated house made of aluminum.

"First I thought, what would we do with aluminum? But the fellow finally convinced me that the house would be good for us and that it would be good for everybody to find out what experience one can have with aluminum in the tropics. So I told him: 'Yes, and thanks.'

"Then they said: 'You know, of course, you only have to make the foundation, but that is a trifle.' Then they gave me the blueprints. Just to read them was a nightmare for me. I am so used to building without plans. But then they told me that the foundation did not have to fit to the exact millimeter. Some story that was! If I'd not had a doctor who was knowledgeable about construction, I would have had to give up the thing at the start. But I had to work at that foundation for weeks and weeks. I who swore never to build again!

"When the contractor from the Swiss firm arrived, he complimented us by saying that he never saw foundations for his houses so exact as ours. That made us almost proud.

"So this became building project number two, and I have to admit that the building was important because I did not really have enough space for all my patients. We have about three hundred and fifty *couchettes,* or mats covered with straw and a blanket. On these they sleep well enough, but there aren't enough of them. Because we have so many patients, I decided to agree to that aluminum building. This is the one that has worried me most and completing it has taken months. But when I left Africa, all was going well, and a fortnight ago I got the message that it is finished. How well an aluminum building fares in the tropics we shall soon see.

"Now to building number three. I could ask you to guess what I might be referring to, and no one would. Could you imagine what else we would need in Lambaréné? No one knows? Well, I did not know it either. A building for an automobile, a Mercedes Benz truck weighing five and a half tons, imagine that! How did such a thing come about, and why?

"You might think that we got high-hatted, that the hospital became big and that we got proud and modern, but those who know me know that the danger of my becoming too modern is not great. But necessity stepped in, namely, the problem of feeding the hospital patients and of being sure that we always had enough to eat. We have to have twenty-seven tons of rice on hand in advance, because there may be months when no shipment comes from Saigon. At least that was always my working principle, to have that much rice on hand.

"But suddenly in the year 1958, no rice is forthcoming. I asked in Lambaréné: 'What is this? No rice has come. Are there no ships bringing rice from Saigon?' They answered me: 'Oh, be calm, *Monsieur.* It will come. This is Africa. Don't worry. It will come. You must have patience. It does not come just when you wish, but it will come.' So I kept my patience, as they had advised. Oh, yes. But one sack of rice was eaten up and then another and another and another. Finally I said: 'What is this? We have only enough left for another week. What will happen?' So I went again to the officials in Lambaréné, and again they answered: 'Don't worry. It will come. It will come.'

145 &

"But I'd heard enough of that. No, I thought, this is a time when more exact information is needed, and I found out that through political circumstances the rice traffic had been interrupted. Saigon had left the business pact with France, and did not accept payments in French money any more. It wanted dollars. You can imagine that we did not have too many dollars around. Anyway, we could not count any more on a regular supply from Saigon. The day had come when I had to admit that I had not enough food for my people. What could I do?

"I went to the local administrator and said: 'Listen. I have no more food for my people. I want to give up my hospital. Half of my patients I will send away, and the other half I will bring to you, and you must feed them and care for them.' This did it. The man finally understood what it all meant and he answered: 'What can we do, *cher Docteur?*' Then I replied that the only alternative was for him to put a car at my disposal so that I could get to villages and buy bananas for my people. He said: 'But certainly, of course, absolutely, Docteur.' And he finally sent a car. So we had to change our staple from rice to bananas, a very serious thing.

"How does the banana market operate in the tropics? In the old times, while the hospital was small, we had almost enough bananas. They were delivered to us by riverway. But not from down the river, only from up the river. This is because one cannot expect the men to paddle upstream with a heavy load of bananas. They can paddle back upstream *after* unloading the bananas. But with this system we were not getting enough bananas. Then the Government built a road linking Libreville and Lambaréné because they also needed bananas from the villages, where there are lots of plantations. One cannot expect the indigènes to carry bananas on the paths through the jungle to the Lambaréné hospital, because bananas are very heavy. Another disadvantage is that they spoil quickly and so cannot be stored for long. In fact, after four days in the tropics they start to rot. So I stood facing the problem, 'How can I get hold of enough bananas quickly and steadily?'

"After a week my great friend, the administrator, decided that I had used his car long enough. He said that he needed it for other projects. My luck had run out. But there was a native who did have a car, and I told him I would make an agreement with him. I said: 'On Thursday you drive from the hospital about twenty miles to those villages which sell bananas. I will send a nurse along with you. She will take along a scale to weigh the bananas, and help you load and unload!' That was fine, he told me, and so we made a contract. But one thing I forgot—to examine the car.

"European people from Lambaréné came to me and said: 'Docteur—how can you send your nurses off in a car which may burst into flames at any moment? It is a dangerous thing, and how its brakes ever work not even the Good Lord knows.' I also realized that no such car would ever solve the problem permanently since we now required eight tons of bananas a week. What we obviously needed was a truck. But the road was not strong enough for a truck so we also needed a new road. And a road that would hold even after heavy rains. At that point the connecting link to the government road was only a narrow path; moreover, it mounted to a steep hill.

"So I had to build a road, and that turned out to be one of my biggest adventures. I even confessed to myself: 'This you can't do.' And in truth it was most unlikely that I could ever finish it because the road had to be widened about two and a half meters, and the foundation had to be filled in to about one meter, and the earth had to be carried by my good workmen.

"But they are not favorably inclined to shovel tons of earth. Not very enthusiastic, at first they had to carry heavy earth for about half a kilometer, and the soil was wet besides. So you can see the beginning was one of the most difficult performances I started in Lambaréné. At first the indigènes really did not want to co-operate. We also had to hew the stones out of the ground, carry them onto the road, and stones that were too big we had to crush with a hammer. I told myself: 'Now, I, myself, will have to stand for at least four months to supervise this job.' I who promised myself never to build again! I who had vowed to do only the hospital work from now on!

"But at this point a miracle happened, a genuine miracle. A Volkswagen appeared on the horizon. Now a Volkswagen has a good reputation. Half of the cars which travel through the Sahara are Volkswagens. It's one of the few cars than can travel through sand. Anyway, from this Volkswagen four youths from Hamburg emerged, one of them slightly injured from an accident in a ditch. We took good care of him, and his companions walked through the hospital, looking very interested. They watched us work, and it was not long before they said to me: 'Docteur, we have seen how hard you work, and we've decided to stay a while and help you build that road.'

"They took the tools and started to hew the big stones from morning till night, and the ambition of these German fellows had a most infectious effect on the indigènes. They became different people and started to work, as though it were fun. The spark took, and in three months we finished that road. It is a great road, sweeping behind the hospital in a big turn, and it rises to a hill of about thirty meters, and it serves well. Now the big question was, What kind of automobile would be most useful? I held a meeting of mechanics and asked them. Unanimously, they replied: 'A Mercedes-Benz, five-and-a-half ton diesel.'

" 'Perhaps that is right,' I thought. I had just read a report that the President of the French Republic and the German Chancellor had embraced each other at a political meeting so I figured the time was ripe to buy a German car even if living in a French territory. You see how wonderful it is when two people suddenly start up a friendship which no one would have expected! Anyway, I was lucky again. I contacted the Mercedes firm, and they delivered me the truck for a truly Christian price, I must say.

"And so all is in order. The truck travels well on the new road; once a week it brings us about eight tons of bananas. Thus we've become independent of the arrival of rice. I need rice only for the summer months when bananas are more scarce. So fifteen tons of rice suffice. And that is how my hospital has entered the modern age. But one thing I will guarantee you, modern times will not alter the old spirit of modesty and economy, the spirit of small beginnings. In this spirit the hospital developed, and in this spirit it shall live on."

Finally, the day of the screening of our film arrives. It is to be seen by Dr. Schweitzer, and by the people of Günsbach, many of whom have known him since his childhood but have never seen his hospital and home in Lambaréné. The baker, the shoemaker, the cobbler, the teacher, the postman—these are the people who will never be able to visit him in Africa to see it for themselves.

I am both terribly excited and apprehensive. After long years of work, the goal has been reached. But how will he, the Doctor himself, react?

I have suggested to Dr. Schweitzer earlier in the week that the drummer of Günsbach, who still announces news to the village population just as in medieval times, tell the town the day and time of the showing, but Schweitzer laughingly put his hand over my mouth.

"Hush," he said. "I am an old man now. Never before was it necessary to let the drummer of Günsbach call the people together on my account. Do you think I want to start such nonsense now? No. That can wait until I die."

"But, Docteur," I pleaded. "How will anybody know that we're showing the film in Münster. I don't want an empty movie house."

"Have no fear," he answered. "The people will come. We will employ the best old system—by word of mouth. But no announcement in the paper, no means of modern communication for me."

And so it was. I told the postman. The postman told the mayor. And the word got around. Whenever I saw a group of people huddled together, I could be sure of hearing them mention the great day of the premiere of the Doctor's film in Münster, Haut Rhin, his home, his valley, his country. We have picked a Saturday evening because Dr. Schweitzer said it was a night when everybody could stay up a bit later than usual.

The cinema in Münster has opened only a few months before. It is a modern building with a seating capacity of about five hundred. I have already tried out the reels and the sound with the projectionist, and feel reasonably sure that the screening and sound will come through clearly. We are using the German version of the film which Dr. Schweitzer narrated himself.

The performance is scheduled for nine o'clock in the evening. At dinner in Günsbach, I am much too excited to eat. One cannot say the same of the Doctor. He eats heartily and scolds me for having no appetite.

"I cannot understand anyone saying no to such delicious food," he tells me. "Come on, Erica. Calm yourself. If people walk out while the film is running, I will console you. I am with you. Don't be nervous."

But his kind words have no effect on me. It is actually *his* judgment that I am most nervous about. Will he now conclude that I have taken up too much of his time all these years and produced nothing worth while?

Looking out the window, I notice more traffic than usual on the road to Münster. Trucks, bicycles, and hay wagons are rolling along in that direction. Will the people in these vehicles be our audience?

Mme. Martin and others from the Günsbach household are wearing their black silk dresses.

"Ready, everybody?" I ask right after dinner.

"I must answer one more letter before we go," Schweitzer declares.

"Please let's go," I beg. "I want you to have a good seat."

"Don't worry about that," Schweitzer replies. "They will have reserved a seat of honor for me, and that's precisely what I do not like. That's why I want to get there late. I want to sit among the townsfolk. I am one of them."

As usual, he wins. I have to bite my tongue and wait.

Finally, by a quarter after eight, I get everybody into the car. Not a single light in the village of Günsbach is on.

"They sure are saving electricity tonight," Dr. Schweitzer jokes. "You'll see. They've all gone to the cinema. You have started something, Erica. You've seduced my good old village into the luxuries of city life. Movies now on Saturday night! Where will it end?"

When we reach Münster, the bells of the church are ringing.

"We'll get out here and walk to the cinema," Schweitzer says. "I don't want to drive up to the door, like some celebrated statesman."

I park the car under the linden trees in the square, and we walk over to the movie house where it seems that the entire population of the Münster Valley has turned up.

"Let's go in the back door," Schweitzer says, looking as if he's been seized by a sudden attack of stage fright. But the auditorium is packed, and when Schweitzer appears, the entire crowd rises and bursts into a roar of applause. This results in Schweitzer's turning right around on his heels and fleeing out the door.

I make after him.

"Docteur! Docteur!" I call. "Please come back. They mean well. What's the matter? Why are you running off? People applaud so often when you appear, aren't you used to it yet?"

"It's different here," Schweitzer replies, hiding behind a row of trees in the dark, outside the building. "These are my friends, my neighbors. You go in, Erica. Tell them that I won't go back unless they stop clapping and unless I can sit way back in the balcony, not on that seat they've reserved for me. Eh? And I see that many people are being turned away, so tell them that a couple more kids can sit on my knees. Only under these conditions will I come back."

I deliver Dr. Schweitzer's message to his friends, but in response, they only laugh and clap again.

"You know him," I shout. "You know that the Alsatian stubbornness in him is strong. You better give in and follow his instructions or I will never get him back."

"All right! All right! We will do what he wants," they call out in chorus, and I go outside to bring the Doctor back.

This time he walks up to the balcony, nodding right and left, shaking hands, picking up one boy and a small girl to hold on his knees. People are already jammed together, two to a seat, but he squeezes in among them and seems happy to have the load on his knees. The owner of the cinema then appears and announces that the film will be run again after the first performance so that no one who has come that night will miss it.

"And in the meantime serve them coffee, on me!" Schweitzer calls out. Then turning to me, he says, laughing: "See now. You don't have to be nervous. Your film will be shown at least *once* more, whatever the verdict is!"

The house lights go out. I stand in the aisle, next to the row in which Schweitzer sits. The music starts, and Dr. Schweitzer's voice booms from the loudspeaker the opening words: *"I was born in the year 1875 in the little town of Kaysersberg in Upper Alsace . . ."* On the screen the house with the little tower appears. A movement goes through the audience. They recognize the place. This part of the Doctor's life is theirs too, they shared it with him. They listen to him recount the years of his childhood, his student days, and the decision to leave his homeland for service in Africa. I watch Dr. Schweitzer's face looking up at the screen, reliving his life. He seems particularly moved when he sees photographs of his father and mother and hears his own confession: *"They educated us for freedom. My father was my dearest friend."* The film rolls on. We see Dr. Schweitzer taking the trip from Bordeaux to Africa, and as the scene appears when his patients welcome him back to the hospital, I know all is well. The audience is with us.

Schweitzer takes us through his hospital, introduces his helpers, the natives, the sick and the well, his animals, his jungle. Watching him again, I see his face light up when the antelopes appear; the antics of his wild pig make him laugh out loud.

We wander with him to the building site where he has constructed his leper village. We go along when, in the evening, he plays the piano. I watch other faces in the audience. When the last pictures fade out on the screen, they burst into applause. There is no holding them back. Schweitzer turns to me and says:

"This time it is for you, Erica."

But I know it is the man and his life to whom the applause of the people of the Vosges Mountains is addressed. They have seen their Doctor in Africa, in another part of the world they will never reach. They have seen him being himself, as he always is, whether in Europe or in Africa, whether he is philosopher, preacher, physician, or artist. And they understand his work better now, after seeing for themselves the haven he has established for those in pain.

When we leave the cinema, the projectionist is loading up for the second performance. Again each seat has to hold two people. In the back of the car, I love hearing each one talk about some scene in the film which has been of particular interest to him.

When we reach the house, Schweitzer sits down and takes my hand.

"Our film is finished," he says. "It will go into the world and tell people of my life after I am gone. I think you have done well. Yes. It is a long way from the time when I wrote, 'I would rather burn in hell than have a film made of my life.' It was good that you were stubborn and pursued your goal. Yes. The film is finished. But our friendship shall continue."